GET READY! GET SET! WORSHIP!

GET READY! GET SET! WORSHIP!

A Resource for Including Children in Worship
for Pastors, Educators, Parents, Sessions, and Committees

by
Sue Lou
Jean Floyd Love
Mickey Meyers
Sylvia Washer

G
GENEVA

Geneva Press
Louisville, Kentucky

First published in 1992 by Sharing Tree Publications, Houston, Texas

Library of Congress Cataloging-in-Publication Data

Lou, Sue.
    Get ready! get set! worship! : a resource for including children
in worship : for pastors, educators, parents, sessions, and
committees / by Sue Lou … [et al.].
        p.   cm.
    Originally published: Houston, Tex. : Sharing Tree Publications,
1992.
    ISBN 0-664-50006-4 (alk. paper)
    1. Children in public worship — Presbyterian Church.   2. Worship
(Religious Education)   3. Presbyterian Church — Liturgy — Study and
teaching.   I. Title.
BV26.2.L68   1997
264'.051'0083 — dc21   97-27904

Clip Art from *Clip Art for Celebrations and Service* by Gertrud Nelson. Copyright © 1987 Pueblo Publishing Company, Inc., © 1990 by The Order of St. Benedict, Inc. Published by The Liturgical Press, Collegeville, Minnesota. Used with permission.

Our appreciation to Gertrud Nelson for adaptations of select pieces of clip art used in "Lord's Prayer with Motions" and "Order of Worship Strips."

TABLE OF CONTENTS

FROM THE WRITERS

We are four church educators who have worked in a variety of Presbyterian churches. In our attempts to meet the challenge of preparing children and families for worship and meaningful participation in the sacraments, we have created a variety of teaching-learning resources. We have used and refined these resources over the years and have found keen interest in them around the church.

We believe we have something special to share with the church. Our collection of studies, learning centers, games, and resources offers short and long term options. It is ready to use and adaptable for all churches — small or large, with or without professional staff. While this material is written from the perspective of the Reformed tradition and targeted for use in Presbyterian churches, it is adaptable for use by other denominations.

Our materials are designed around these beliefs:

1. **Worship is the response of the whole people of God—and that includes children!**
2. **Children learn to worship by worshiping, but we still have responsibility for instructing and nurturing them in the process.**
3. **Parents, pastors, and congregations need assistance, support, and encouragement in their efforts to minister to children.**
4. **The good news is that as growth and change happen for children and families in the practice and understanding of worship, everyone is enriched and energized.**

Our hope is that this book will inform, enhance and encourage the church in its vital ministry with children.

TIPS FOR USING THIS BOOK

This book is designed to be "user friendly." That is to say, all the resources, patterns, and games are ready to copy and use. A few words may be necessary about preparation details.

A Word About Adult Studies

Because any change in worship routine affects everyone in a congregation, it is essential that prayerful thought and study be involved before changes are made. Four adult studies are provided to facilitate this process. Each congregation will decide who should be involved in the studies. What is vital is that Sessions be included as thoughts and plans evolve, and that any new practices be interpreted to the congregation well before implementation.

A Word About Learning Centers

Because children learn best by being actively involved in the process, many learning centers and games are employed in these materials. The learning center approach is used primarily in the Worship Education section in Model I.

Learning centers tend to invite the learner to

—come and see
—come and do
—come and learn

The centers divide a classroom in such a way that children are allowed to make choices, to move about freely, and to pursue their own learning. Learners of different ages can work at the same time, alone, or helping each other. Each can learn at his or her own pace and level, while remaining part of the group.

A Word About Making the Games

Games are provided throughout the material as ways to reinforce learning. The games are ready to reproduce and mount on colored poster board. Laminating or covering with clear contact paper will render them more durable. All the games can be played using either a spinner or a die. These game pieces, spinners, and other necessary materials may be purchased from a school supply store or recycled from commercial games. A fun way to let children make their own pieces is to use "Shrink Art" (See Church Year Idea). Games are designed to be played by three to four children. You will need several copies of each game if your group is large.

A Word About Copying the Resources

If resources or games are too small for little children to use, these pages may be enlarged on a copy machine with "enlarging" capability.

PART 1
ADULT STUDY

AN ADULT STUDY: INTRODUCTION

This is a four-session study designed to be used in a variety of ways. Some of these may be with parents of young children, with the Worship and Christian Education committees, with the Session, or with a group representing all of the above. The study may utilize the leadership of the pastor, the church educator, and elders.

Each of the studies is designed to take about an hour, so they are appropriate for the church school time frame or for other times.

Most Presbyterian congregations have children and youth as a part of their worshiping communities. But few have given thought to what that fact means within the life of the congregation. Those who have planned ways for children and youth to be appropriately included report that the whole congregation has benefited.

The Presbyterian Church (U.S.A.) welcomes baptized children to the Lord's Table. Some Presbyterian churches simply ignore this fact, others take it as a serious responsibility to help parents educate their children.

The purpose of this study is to find ways to make the worship experience and the sacraments more meaningful and inclusive for the variety of ages in the worshiping community.

Objectives for Participants:

1. To be informed as to what the Reformed tradition and the Bible tell us regarding children in the worship experience

2. To explore what it is we want to happen in the worship experience for all participants

3. To look at the issues surrounding children in the worship experience

4. To ponder the central understandings of the sacraments from the Reformed perspective

5. To examine what our denomination is teaching children about worship and the sacraments

6. To suggest what your church might do to better help parents in teaching their children about the sacraments and worship

SESSION ONE:
THINKING ABOUT WORSHIP

PURPOSE:

To put participants in touch with the memory of their childhood experiences of worship. To put adults in touch with their expectations concerning the worship experience. To examine what the Bible and our denomination say about worship.

TO PREPARE:

Provide pencils, paper, Bibles, and copies of "Worship for All God's People" (Adult Resource 1) which includes references from the *Book of Order*. Post pictures of worship on all walls.

1. As the group arrives, have pictures suggesting worship displayed around the room (stained glass windows, people at prayer, churches, etc.). Ask the participants to walk around and look at the pictures, recalling some of their childhood memories of worship. Ask each person to find a partner, someone other than a family member. Have the partners interview each other by sharing some of their memories and be ready to introduce their partner to the group. The leader should record words and phrases that highlight what is said.

2. The leader then asks the participants to think of words that tell how the children in your church seem to feel during your worship. What are the areas of concern this conversation raises? The leader will point out that often we are unaware that some of our feelings about worship are a result of our expectations. Invite the group to list some expectations they have as they come to worship (quiet, order, respect, no interruptions, etc.). Discuss how these expectations set the tone for worship in your congregation (i.e., if the adults expect that worship will be quiet and uninterrupted, it will be difficult for young children to feel welcome).

3. The leader hands out copies of "Worship for All God's People" and reviews the contents.

4. Assign passages to be read, looking for applications to worship in your congregation.

BIBLE PASSAGES	BOOK OF ORDER	
I Cor. 12:12–27	W. 1.4003	(These passages from the *Book of Order* are
Deut. 31:11–13	W. 1.4007	included in "Worship for All God's People")
Matt. 18:1–5	W. 3.1004	
Joshua 4:19–24	W. 3.3201	
	W. 5.7002	
	W. 6.2006	

After individual studies have been done, share and record the responses. Which of the things you have listed are already being done well in your congregation? Which ones need more work?

5. Close with prayer.

ship for All God's People

The call to worship is addressed to all.

Worship is the central act of the gathered community of God. It is something the people of God do in response to God and God's acts of love on our behalf. Through worship, people attend to the presence of God in their lives. Our *Book of Order* (W-1.4.003) expresses it this way: "In Jesus Christ, the Church is a royal priesthood in which worship is the work of everyone. The people of God are called to participate in the common ministry of worship. No one shall be excluded from participation or leadership in public worship in the Lord's house on the grounds of race, color, class, age, sex, or handicapping condition."

The worship experience is essential for the formation of identity as people of God. John Westerhoff has alerted us to the fact that it is through worship that the church passes on its understandings and its ways. In fact, Westerhoff makes a number of bold affirmations about the essential importance of including children in worship:

—If our children are to have faith, they must worship with us.

—Not only is the content of our faith communicated but also the feelings, subtle nuances, and transcendent meanings are learned through participation.

Carolyn Hardin Englehardt, director of the Paul Vieth Resource Center at Yale Divinity School, says that the reason worship is so important is that, "one participates his or her way into the faith community. One is shaped by the liturgy in which one participates. One is shaped without necessarily knowing it and without necessarily being able to explain what is happening. No other aspect of the life of the congregation can provide this experience of being formed into the community of faith." The *Book of Order* states, "The life of the Christian flows from the worship of the church, where identity as a believer is confirmed and where one is commissioned to a life of discipleship and of personal response to God" (W-5.1001).

Children are, by their baptism, members of the people of God. Baptism is the sign and symbol of inclusion in God's grace and covenant with the Church. Baptism signifies adoption into the covenant family of the Church (W-2.3004).

In *The Public Worship of God* Henry Sloane Coffin affirms, "Worship is the offering to God of the entire congregation of his people, and children should certainly be included. A childless congregation presents an abnormal and unpromising appearance."

The *Book of Order* (W-3.1004) speaks to the inclusion of children:

"Children bring special gifts to worship and grow in the faith through their regular inclusion and participation in the worship of the congregation. Those responsible for planning and leading the participation of children in worship should consider the children's level of understanding and ability to respond, and should

(continued)

avoid both excessive formality and condescension."

The guidance offered in the *Book of Order* (W-3.3201) for the ordering of worship is:

> "In setting an order of worship on the Lord's Day, the pastor with the concurrence of the session shall provide opportunity for people from youngest to oldest to participate in a worthy offering of praise to God and for them to hear and to respond to God's Word."

Lucie Barber in *Religious Education of Preschoolers* supports this emphasis on the inclusion of children by saying, "The worship service is where faithing is experienced. Children must have the opportunity to function side by side with adults in the worshiping community if they are to realize their gifts as members of the body."

Children learn to value corporate worship only by being a part of inclusive worship on a regular basis. Children model adults. By observing parents and others at worship, children learn words, attitudes, postures, and feelings of the community. Worship is the great ritual of our faith, and as such is powerful in shaping our lives.

The key role of parents is noted in paragraph W-5.7002 of the *Book of Order*:

> "The parent(s) or the one(s) exercising parental responsibility should teach their children about Christian worship by example, by providing for household worship, and by discussion and instruction. . . . "

So we affirm: Children learn to worship by worshiping.

The Church affirms: Worship can be and should be nurtured by education.

The *Book of Order* has some clear instructions about the importance of education:

W-1.4007: "In the exercise of its responsibility to encourage the participation of its people in worship, the session should provide for education in Christian worship by means appropriate to the age, interests, and circumstances of the members of the congregation."

W-3.1004: "The session should insure that regular programs of the church do not prevent children's full participation with the whole congregation in worship, in Word and Sacrament, on the Lord's Day."

W-6.2006: "The central occasion for nurture in the church is the Service for the Lord's Day, when the Word is proclaimed and the Sacraments are celebrated. All members of the community, from oldest to youngest, are encouraged to be present and to participate. Educational activities should not be scheduled which prevent regular participation in this service."

SESSION TWO: BAPTISM

PURPOSE:

To be informed about the sacrament of baptism for infants/children and its implications for congregational life. To consider the meaning of the baptismal vows for congregational life.

TO PREPARE:

Make copies of the "Baptism Mixer" (Adult Resource #2) for each person.

1. As people arrive, ask them to play the "Baptism Mixer" game. Discuss the game, asking what the group learned about each other and about the symbols of baptism. Does your congregation have any special baptismal traditions?

2. Use the "Sacrament of Baptism" (Adult Resource #2) material to lead the group in a discussion, or use the following questions to reflect on the gift of baptism.

   A. Think about belonging. Name some of the places where you really belong. How does it feel to belong? What kinds of things let you know you belong—gestures, words, symbols? Share your thoughts with another person and then as a group. What is it that gives children (and you) the feeling that you really belong to the community of God's people?

   B. What comes to mind when you think about what you have been told or what you remember about your own baptism?

   C. Recall a recent baptism at your church. What feelings and thoughts are triggered in you when you participate in this sacrament? What meanings does the experience have for the nurture of the child by parents and congregation?

   D. What feelings are evoked for you when you remember your own baptism and declare, "I am baptized!"?

3. When our denomination acted to welcome baptized children to the Lord's Table, a new issue was presented to congregations. Some of our families, for whatever reasons, had not had their children baptized as infants. Since only those children who have been baptized are to be invited to the Lord's Table, parents of unbaptized children have some

decisions to make. What can the church do to help these families understand the issues and support them in their decision? Here are some possibilities:

A. Offer an instructional class on baptism for parents and children.

B. Plan appropriate services of baptism with families who choose to have their child baptized.

C. Discuss with any parents who choose not to have their child baptized how they can best help their child understand that he or she will wait until confirmation and baptism to begin to participate in the Sacrament of Communion.

4. Close with this version of the congregation's baptismal vow:

"Do you, as members of the church of Jesus Christ,
promise to guide and nurture N. and N.
by word and deed,
with love and prayer,
encouraging *them* to know and follow Christ
and to be faithful *members* of his church?"

Book of Common Worship (WJKP, 1993), 406

Adult Resource #2

Sacrament of Baptism

In baptism, we affirm that the person — infant, child, or adult — belongs to the community of faith. It is a rite of belonging. Walter Brueggemann in *Belonging and Growing in the Christian Community* (CE:SA *Living the Word Resource*) speaks of belonging as one of the deep mysteries of our human experience. And we all have a yearning to belong. This is true of children, particularly kindergarten and elementary age children. They want and need to belong, to be known and valued. "The good news of the gospel," says Brueggemann, "is about belonging. It is about belonging in a caring community of covenant with God and with sisters and brothers who participate in that covenant. The task of this community is to share this good news with others — to welcome them and to nurture them, young and old alike."

The community Brueggemann speaks of exists due to God's initiative and love. It is God who creates, sustains, and empowers the community of faith. God calls us into relationship before we are even aware of the relationship. God's love precedes our ability to respond. Baptism is God's gift. Harold M. Daniels puts it this way:

"We all should receive God's gift of new life just as naturally as a baby receives nourishment, love, and care from its parent. A mother and father do not wait until their baby understands before they lovingly cuddle her and speak to her. Love is not withheld until she can return it. Parents do not wait to choose a name until their baby is old enough to choose a name. Parents give a name, and share the family name with their baby, hoping that the child will grow up proudly bearing the name they gave and the family name into which she was born.

"So also in Baptism, God's unmerited love is evidenced. The child is born into the household of faith, and now bears a new family name, the name of the triune God. The church prays that the child will grow up proudly bearing the family name into which he or she is baptized and will make the Christian faith his or her own." (*Worship in the Community of Faith* by The Joint Office of Worship, Louisville, 64–65).

Baptism signifies one's entrance into the family of God. We are baptized into the community of faith, and we are dependent upon the community for our nurture and growth in faith. Catherine Gunsalus Gonzalez likens baptism to birth — birth into the people of God, and, like birth, it is once and for all. But each time we participate in the Sacrament of Baptism we are committing ourselves to the other. So we live out our baptism by caring for others (*A Theology of the Lord's Supper*).

The church requires that parents or guardians of the infant being baptized provide assurance that the child will be nurtured in the faith and that faith will have an opportunity to grow in the life of the child. The church also requires the whole congregation to take part in the baptism and to promise to nurture, love, and assist the infant to be a faithful disciple.

SESSION THREE: COMMUNION

PURPOSE:
To focus on the meaning of the Sacrament of Communion.

TO PREPARE:
Have a gift box containing a chalice (goblet) and a loaf of bread inside. Make copies of "Sacrament of Communion" (Adult Resource #3) and "Responsibilities" (Adult Resource #4).

1. Ask everyone to get a partner and sit next to them. One person is "A" and the other one is "B". Ask the "A"s to tell their partners all the reasons they can think of for allowing children to take Communion. Ask the "B"s to tell their partners all the reasons they can think of for not allowing children to take Communion. After a few minutes, ask each team of partners to summarize their reasons and list these statements for all the group to see. The leader may want to have two columns, one for and one against children participating in the Lord's Supper.

2. A. Bring out the gift box. Open it, remove elements and display them. Say, "One understanding of the Sacrament of Communion is that it focuses on the gifts of Jesus Christ. Each time we celebrate Communion, we receive that gift and we remember. We must never lose sight of the fact that Communion *is* God's gift to us, not something which "mature Christians" are entitled to because they understand its meaning.

   B. Use the "Sacrament of Communion" to do one of the following: 1) Cut paragraphs apart and have a participant read each paragraph. 2) Have someone do a short presentation of the material. 3) Make copies of the material and ask everyone to read and comment on it.

   C. Form three small groups. Give each group one of the following sections:

      1) What cultures do you know where bread is a basic food for survival? Is it easier for Christians in those cultures to understand the symbolism of bread for the sustaining of spiritual life?

      2) In what ways is blood a symbol for life? How do you handle the concept of "drinking blood" with children who are literal-minded and very interested in gory stories? (See "Sacrament of Communion: A One-Hour Session Outline, Part 3").

      3) Share a memory of giving or receiving a gift. Put yourself in God's place and consider how you would want the church to receive and respond to the gift of Communion. Why is remembering a key factor in one's expectations of Communion?

   Discuss and be prepared to share with the whole group.

3. List what your congregation is currently doing to make sure its children are prepared to

come to the Lord's Table. Look at the copies of "Responsibilities." Are parents being reminded of their responsibilities? What is the Session doing in regard to its responsibilities? Session Four of this Adult Study is called "Making Plans." Encourage the group to begin thinking and praying now about what some of your church's new plans might be.

4. Close with prayer.

Sacrament of Communion

The sacraments are gifts of God to assure us of God's love. They have been called "heavenly mysteries." Maria Harris in *Teaching and Religious Imagination* defines mystery this way: "A mystery is not that about which we cannot know anything, but that about which we cannot know everything. Mystery is that before which the natural, human and appropriate response is awe and that which provokes, fascinates and draws us in." In other words, we never fully understand the sacraments, but each time we participate in either of them, we unwrap the gift afresh as Word connects with life experience.

Communion/the Lord's Supper is the gift that focuses us on the gift of Jesus Christ. So each time the Lord's Supper is celebrated we receive Christ's gift and we remember. We are also reminded that Christ is asking us to be obedient and faithful to doing God's will in our lives and in the world.

Like the early church we sense that this gift/mystery is not to be taken lightly. One lingering concern about children's participation in the sacrament is their ability to "discern."

Let's look at what was going on in the early church that prompted Paul's admonition about "discerning the body" (1 Cor. 11:29). The practice of the early church was to gather for a meal around which they celebrated the Lord's Supper. The Corinthian church was so divided that they didn't even eat together. Those with plenty ate and drank to excess while "those who had nothing were humiliated" (1 Cor. 11:22b). Paul declared that they were not celebrating the Lord's Supper because they did not understand what it meant to be the body of Christ. To be the body means that every single part is needed and valued equally (1 Cor. 12:24-25). Paul's word about "discerning the body" in this passage is that whatever fractures the community profanes the body and blood of the Lord. Arlo Duba (*Worship in the Community of Faith*, p. 109) says, "Could it be that to leave out someone who has been baptized into the one body is part of what Paul means by failure to discern the body? By extension, I believe that our children should not be left out. The covenant promise is to you and your children (Acts 2:39), for by their baptism they are a part of the body, the covenant community."

Our *Book of Order* (W 2.4011b) provides this word of guidance to the church regarding children: "Baptized children who are being nurtured and instructed in the significance of the invitation to the Table and the meaning of their response are invited to receive the Lord's Supper, recognizing that their understanding of participation will vary according to their maturity."

David Ng (*The Austin Seminary Bulletin*, October, 1978) expressed it this way: "Children are a part of the covenant community of the Body of Christ. Their full participation in this Body helps the community to realize its wholeness; without children the church is less of a church. . . . Their presence and participation in communion help to make this sacrament much more of a communion."

(continued)

That which we commonly refer to as Communion is known by many names, and each name carries with it a dimension of the sacrament's meaning. *The Book of Common Worship* of the Presbyterian Church (U.S.A.) points this out: "The many-faceted meaning of this sacrament is seen in the names given to it. The title *Lord's Supper* recalls Jesus' institution of the sacrament with his disciples. *Eucharist* (thanksgiving) reminds us that we receive all of the benefits of God's grace with joy. *Holy Communion* reminds us that in this sacrament we are made one with Christ and with each other. *The Breaking of the Bread* describes the sacramental action by which Christ is known to his disciple" (*Book of Common Worship*, Westminster John Knox Press, 1992).

Responsibilities as a Parent

To present my child for baptism (G 5.0202).

To model authentic faith and worship (set a Godly example).

To tell the stories of the faith and provide information for my child.

To provide opportunities for experience of worship.

To act as a consultant—that is, helping my child to ask questions and seek answers.

To exercise parental responsibility for sharing the faith of the church with children (W 6.2005).

To strive to bring up my child to love and serve God.

To prepare my baptized child for participation in the Lord's Supper (W 4.2002).

To decide when my child will participate in the Sacrament of the Lord's Supper.

Responsibilities of the Session with Regard to Children at the Table

1. Provide pastoral care and instruction of the church (G 5.0201).

2. Maintain a roll of baptized members [G10.0302a (1)].

3. Encourage parents to present children for baptism and instruct parents as to the meaning of the sacrament (W 2.3012).

4. Counsel the families under its care to prepare their baptized children for participation in the Lord's Supper. The Session shall equip and support the parent(s) or those exercising parental responsibility for their task of nurturing the child for receiving the Lord's Supper (W 4.2002).

5. Invite, through the minister, baptized children who are being nurtured and instructed to participate, with an understanding of the significance of the invitation to the Lord's Table and of their response in faith (W 2.4011).

6. Encourage baptized children and their parents or guardian to participate in public worship and in the Sacrament of the Lord's Supper (W 3.1004 & G 5.0201).

References: *Book of Order* (The Constitution of the Presbyterian Church [U.S.A.], Part II).

SESSION FOUR: MAKING PLANS

PURPOSE:

To explore ways to make worship more meaningful for all the children of the congregation.

TO PREPARE:

Title four sheets of newsprint "Children up to Age Four," "Children Four to Six," "Children Six to Ten," "Children Eleven to Fourteen." Post these around the room and provide washable markers for writing. Leave room for an extra sheet of newsprint to be added next to each "Children" sheet. Have four other sheets ready which are titled "How This Impacts Worship." Have enough index cards available so that each person may have seven. Make copies of "Welcoming Children to Worship" (Adult Resource #5). Assign someone in the class to read ahead and be ready to share information about children's age characteristics. Make copies of "Ways to Involve Children in Congregational Worship" (Part 4).

1. As participants arrive, ask them to write something they know about children in the age categories listed around the room. Begin by reviewing the comments on characteristics of children in the various age groups. Ask the person who has studied the "Welcoming Children to Worship" guide to add to each one, if needed.

2. Post a "How This Impacts Worship" newsprint sheet next to each age-group sheet. List together the specific things now happening during your worship time that could provide for the needs of each age group. Look at "Ways to Involve Children in Congregational Worship" for things you missed.

3. You are moving now toward some final recommendations from your group. Post or write on a board this statement: "What could _____ do to help nurture the faith of children through their participation in congregational worship?" Give each participant a set of seven blank index cards. Ask them to write a heading at the top of each one. The headings are:

   (1) Session
   (2) Worship Committee
   (3) Christian Education Committee
   (4) Pastor
   (5) Church Educator
   (6) Parents and grandparents
   (7) People without children

   Ask each person to write one suggestion for each group using one heading per card. Collect and sort the cards into the seven number groups. Ask someone to summarize and report suggestions for each of the groups. These can be written and given to the Session or the appropriate committees for action.

4. End by reading "Sitting with Lindsey."

Adult Resource #5

Welcoming Children to Worship: A Parent's Guide

Children are a part of the family of the church, so they should be included in the worshiping community. Making their presence a joyful experience for the children, their parents, and those who worship around them, takes care and planning. Much will depend on the age and temperament of the child, for each child is different and needs special consideration.

WHEN A CHILD IS AN INFANT, parents often feel uneasy about leaving their child because of health and care issues. There is no reason not to bring an infant to worship; in fact, this may well be the simplest time to have a child in church. Child development experts tell us that the smells, sounds, and feelings that infants experience as part of worship may help to bond them to the church family.

Families with infants will want to sit in a place where they can leave easily if their child needs attention or becomes fussy. Churches should provide areas for diaper changing and a private place for a mother to nurse a child; and they should make these facilities known to parents of infants, especially those who are visiting.

WHEN CHILDREN ARE TODDLERS, the nursery is usually the best place for them to be. Toddlers need to move and make noise and explore their surroundings. Few are the parents who can successfully and lovingly manage these needs during a worship service. Most parents find it is easier on them and their child to leave the child in the nursery, even if there are some tears when the child is left. If good quality care and a stimulating environment are provided, the tears usually end quickly. If the child care worker reports that the child cannot be comforted, parents may want to try bringing the child into worship with them for a while, or even staying in the nursery for several Sundays until the child is more at home there.

There are certainly some special times when a toddler could enjoy being in worship for at least part of the service. Days like Palm Sunday, Christmas Eve, or other services with lots of color and movement, can be a great joy for a young child.

WHEN CHILDREN ARE IN PRE-KINDERGARTEN OR KINDERGARTEN, it may be possible for them to enjoy the worship service, though most probably still prefer and need to be in the nursery. With help, the child can participate in much of the service by holding the book, standing with the congregation, finding the page, following a few words in the bulletin, or putting an offering envelope in the plate. Coloring or other activities should be saved for the sermon time, when being still and quiet is highly valued by parents and others. If a child cannot handle an entire service, they might stay for the first part and then leave for the nursery at an appropriate time.

Preschoolers may lead the congregation in worship by participating in a children's choir or in special services such as Palm Sunday or Pentecost. They may also participate in the children's sermon.

(continued)

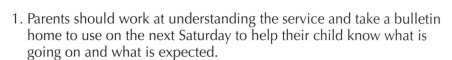

WHEN A CHILD IS IN ELEMENTARY SCHOOL, worship can be a challenge or a joy. There may no longer be child-care programs or classes offered for school-age children, since most congregations plan for worship attendance. This is a good time for parents and children to think and study together about the worship service, and plan for what worship will mean in their family. Here are a few ideas:

1. Parents should work at understanding the service and take a bulletin home to use on the next Saturday to help their child know what is going on and what is expected.

2. Try to avoid making worship attendance a power struggle. Treat it in the same matter-of-fact way that school or other family events are treated. Refuse to be drawn into arguments about worship attendance, by using simple, clear statements, such as: "Our family goes to church."

   Listen to any real issues that children have, and try to help them find ways to deal with these. Try letting your child decide where the family will sit in the sanctuary, what book to bring, what clothes to wear. Give them as much power and responsibility for attending worship as you can.

3. A child may wish to bring a bag with a book to read, paper and crayons, a book of puzzles, or some other things to enjoy during the sermon time. Toys like cars, Barbie dolls, or other games that take space and "sounds" to play, will usually lead to trouble and are best left at home. Nothing fuels the controversy over children in the worship faster than a little boy playing cars under the pew!

4. Elementary children may be involved in worship leadership in many ways. For ideas, see "Ways to Involve Children in Congregational Worship."

SUMMARY: The hope is that worship will be a time of joy for children and their families. But the reality is, sitting still and being quiet does not always give children joy. When children misbehave in worship, parents have to deal with their own feelings of embarrassment and frustration. Many a child has been pinched, threatened, or dragged out screaming, because a parent "lost it" during worship. Planning ahead for what you will do if your child becomes noisy or restless will help you do a better job of managing your frustration. One of the ways we keep the vows we make when our children are baptized is to give thought, effort, and prayer to their participation in worship. Good worship experiences don't "just happen." If children feel loved, included, and accepted in worship it is because both the church and the parents have been faithful to their tasks.

Sitting with Lindsey

She can't read and she hums the hymns, but she's fine company on a Sunday morning.

By Ruth Rex Dorman

Lindsey asked to sit with me again. It's always so gratifying when she does that. I know what it means to me, but what does she get out of it?

Lindsey knows the Order of Worship inside out—up to "The Time with Our Children," when she leaves for Sunday school. She knows whatever is memorizable, and she feels the importance of playing her part in the worship service. Once when the pastor was giving the "Assurance of Pardon" I heard her start to speak, and then stop. Anxious not to miss saying the response but not yet quite sure of her cue, she began to say, "In Jesus Christ we are forgiven" whenever he would pause for breath. Now she confidently waits for "Friends, believe the good news" before she draws a deep breath and sails into her part.

Lindsey can't read, but she mumbles along on the written responses and holds her half of my hymnal while humming along on the hymns. Our favorite is "All Creatures of Our God and King"— there are so many "Alleluias" to belt out. The fact that every now and then an "O sing ye" sneaks in where you'd expect an "Alleluia" only adds spice to the endeavor.

Knowing what's expected during the "Passing of the Peace," Lindsey politely smiles and shakes hands with all the elderly (over 25) people sitting around us. After a decent interval of this, we sit down again and tickle each other in a friendly way until the ministers return to their places—which actually is a very effective and appropriate way to pass the peace. (We know some adults who should try it.)

Lindsey and I always look up the Old Testament reading in the pew Bible. We do this because she so much enjoys being in charge of lifting it out of the rack and also because she is so impressed that I can find the place without a page number. We both feel more holy when we look up the reading.

Lindsey doesn't understand a tenth of what happens while she's in church. I, on the other hand, understand it on a much deeper level because I find myself looking for the meaning and framing explanations that she would understand. She never hears these explanations —we both have a highly developed sense of appropriate behavior. It is not appropriate to talk during the service, and after the service is when you play tag in the garth.

After "The Time With Our Children"—when Lindsey leaves—I find the rest of the service flat. It seems to me it would be much better to have "The Time with Our Children" later in the service—say, after the sermon. As it is, even the "Presentation of Tithes and Offerings" lacks zest because there's no little girl beside me anxiously waiting for the plate with a quarter clutched in her hand.

I feel sorry for people who don't get to sit with Lindsey even for a short time. Have they ever counted off the number of "Alleluias" in "All Creatures of Our God and King?" Do they watch for the wooden flaps over the organ pipes to move when Mrs. Talevich starts the "Gloria Patri?" Does anyone ever tickle them during the "Passing of the Peace?" Tomorrow is Sunday. I hope Lindsey will sit with me again.

———————————————

Ruth Rex Dorman is a member of First Presbyterian Church in Anaheim, Calif. This article first appeared in *Recadero,* the Presbytery of Los Ranchos newsletter. It also appeared in the *Presbyterian Survey* (November 1990). Reprinted with permission from *Presbyterian Survey* and Ruth Rex Dorman.

BIBLIOGRAPHY

CHILDREN AND WORSHIP

A Place for You: Toward the Integration of Children into the Life of the Church. Toronto: United Church of Canada, 1989.

Armstrong, Lance. *Children in Worship: the Road to Faith*. Melbourne: The Joint Board of Christian Education, 1988.

Benton, Jim. *Welcome to Worship: A Guide for Preparing First Graders for Corporate Worship*. St. Louis: Christian Board of Publication.

Brokering, Lois. *Rainbow Bags*. Minneapolis: Augsburg Publishing House, 1986.

Brown, Carolyn C. *Gateways to Worship: A Year of Worship Experiences for Young Children*. Nashville: Abingdon Press, 1989.

Brown, Carolyn C. *Forbid Them Not: Involving Children in Sunday Worship* (Based on the Common Lectionary, Year C). Nashville: Abingdon Press, 1991.

Duckert, Mary. *Together at the Table: Children in the Congregation*. Philadelphia: The Geneva Press, 1981.

Gobbel, Roger and Phillip C. Huber. *Creative Designs with Children at Worship*. Atlanta: John Knox Press, 1981.

Hanson, Richard Simon. *Worshiping with the Child*. Nashville: Abingdon Press, 1988.

Heusser, D-B and Phyllis. *Children as Partners in the Church*. Valley Forge: Judson Press, 1985.

Jansen, John F. *Let Us Worship God: An Interpretation for Families*. Richmond: CLC Press, 1966.

Johnson, Miriam J. *Inside Twenty-five Classic Children's Stories*. New York: Paulist Press, 1986.

Johnson, Miriam J. *Inside Twenty-five More Classic Children's Stories*. New York: Paulist Press.

Johnson, Phillip E. *Celebrating the Seasons with Children* (1984), *More Celebrating the Seasons with Children* (1985), *And More Celebrating the Seasons with Children* (1986). New York: Pilgrim Press.

Juengst, Sara Covin. *Sharing Faith with Children*. Louisville, Ky.: Westminster/John Knox Press, 1994.

Keith-Lucas, Alan. *What We Do in Church*. Chapel Hill, N.C.: University Presbyterian Church.

Lehn, Cornelia. *Involving Children and Youth in Congregational Worship*. Scottdale, Pa.: Mennonite Publishing House, 1982.

McLarty, Phillip W. *The Children, Yes! Involving Children in Our Congregation's Worship*. Nashville: Discipleship Resources, 1981.

Merritt, David, editor. *Seen and Heard, New Possibilities for Children in the Church*. Melbourne, Australia: Joint Board of Christian Education, 1986.

Morris, Margie. *Helping Children Feel at Home in Church*. Nashville: Discipleship Resources, 1988.

Ng, David and Virginia Thomas. *Children in the Worshiping Community*. Atlanta: John Knox Press, 1981.

Peery, Agnes Junkin. *Let All the People: Experiences in Corporate Worship with Children*. Abingdon Presbytery Office, P.O. Box 317, Wytheville, VA 24382.

Smith, W. Allen. *Children Belong in Worship, A Guide to the Children's Sermon*. St. Louis: CSP Press, 1984.

Stewart, Stan, Pauline Stewart and Richard Green. *Going to Church with Children*. Melbourne, Australia: The Joint Board of Christian Education, 1987.

Stewart, Sonja M. and Jerome W. Berryman. *Young Children and Worship*. Louisville: Westminster/John Knox Press, 1990.

Thomas, Virginia and Betty Davis Miller. *Children's Literature for All God's Children*. Atlanta: John Knox Press, 1986.

Westerhoff, John H. III. *A Pilgrim People, Learning through the Church Year*. Minneapolis: The Seabury Press, 1984.

CHILDREN'S BOOKS

Boling, Ruth, Lauren J. Muzzy, Laurie A. Vance. Illustrated by Tracey D. Carrier. *A Children's Guide to Worship*. Louisville, Ky.: Geneva Press, 1998.

Evans, Colleen Townsend. *Teaching Your Child to Pray*. Garden City, N.Y.: Doubleday, 1978.

Fogle, Jeanne S. *Signs of God's Love—Baptism and Communion* (1984) *Symbols of God's Love—Codes and Passwords* (1986). Philadelphia: The Geneva Press.

Turner, Rosalie. *My Very Own Book of the Lord's Prayer*. Nashville: Abingdon Press, 1986.

PART 2
WORSHIP EDUCATION FOR CHILDREN

PREPARING CHILDREN TO PARTICIPATE IN WORSHIP

MODEL I: SESSION OUTLINE

"Find The Church" (Worship Resource #1)

The Sanctuary Game

Sanctuary Outline (Worship Resource #2)

About Learning Centers

Apostles' Creed Learning Center

The Apostles' Creed (Worship Resource #3)

Hymnbook Marker Learning Center

Lord's Prayer Learning Center

The Lord's Prayer (Worship Resource #4)

The Lord's Prayer Guide (Worship Resource #5)

The Lord's Prayer with Motions (Worship Resource #6)

Offering Learning Center

Order of Worship Learning Center

Order of Worship Strips (Worship Resources #7A, B, C, D)

Worship Fold-ups Learning Center

Worship Fold-ups (Worship Resources #8A, B, C, D, E)

MODEL II: SESSION I: WE HAVE A SPECIAL PLACE TO WORSHIP

Suggested Questions for Sanctuary Game (Worship Resource #9)

SESSION 2: WORSHIP IS OUR RESPONSE TO GOD'S LOVE

Doxology (Worship Resource #10)

Psalm 100 (Worship Resource #11)

SESSION 3: WE HAVE A PLAN TO HELP US WORSHIP

SESSION 4: WE PRAY AS A PART OF OUR WORSHIP

Prayer Chart (Worship Resource #12)

The Praying Game (Worship Resource #13)

Educational Models for Worship Education

PREPARING CHILDREN TO PARTICIPATE IN WORSHIP

Children belong in worship! At baptism, we affirm that they are a part of the family of God right now, not "the church of tomorrow."

Having made that affirmation, we must also affirm that the worship hour is often taxing on young children, on their families, and on those around them. Parents may be unrealistic in their expectations of their children's behavior during worship. Their need for the child to be quiet and still may make them forget what their child needs in order to do those things. It is important for the church to provide ways for parents and children to learn about worship. A classroom setting is the best way for this learning to take place, since it offers time to discuss and ask questions.

Here are two models you may choose for working with parents and children to learn more about worship. As children understand what the worship service is and see that they are included, worship is enhanced for everyone. As parents understand their children's needs and abilities, they can become worship partners and not just disciplinarians.

WORSHIP EDUCATION, MODEL I, IS A ONE-HOUR SESSION designed to help children and parents become familiar with the sanctuary and the parts of the worship service of your congregation. The curriculum is written with first and second graders in mind, because it is as first graders that children often begin staying for the entire worship service. This class may be scheduled for August or September, and then followed by the sessions on baptism and Communion. This schedule allows children to be welcomed at the Lord's Table on World Communion Sunday (first Sunday in October).

The class is set up as a series of learning centers. Learning centers are used because they allow children to touch and to interact with concepts of worship which are often intangible to them. Children will learn about the sanctuary, become more familiar with the bulletin, make markers for finding the hymns, learn and grow in their understanding of the Lord's Prayer and Apostles' Creed, and know what happens to the offering. There may be more centers suggested than are reasonable for a small group to do in a one–hour session. This allows you to choose which centers suit your situation best, or even to plan a second class session to cover all the materials.

WORSHIP EDUCATION, MODEL II, CONTAINS FOUR ONE-HOUR SESSIONS focusing on the sanctuary, worship as praise, understanding the bulletin, and prayer. Some of the learning centers suggested for Model I will be used in Model II as well. Both models are structured for use with younger children. If you have a small group of children in elementary classes, they can all work together on these sessions. Older children could be paired with younger ones to do the reading and the learning centers. Or for classes which are broadly graded, particularly in small churches, additional activities are included which are more suitable for older elementary-age children.

These materials may be used in a number of settings. Classes could be at the church school hour, for summer church school classes, for special short-term classes (such as a January term), for Sunday afternoon or weekday evening sessions, or for vacation church school.

Parents are encouraged to attend with their children for several important reasons: 1) Parents need to know what their children are learning about worship so that the family is "on the same track." 2) Parents need to think about how to best help their children be participants in worship. 3) The learning centers require some reading skills, so first and second graders will need a helper. Plus, this is a fun learning experience!

WORSHIP EDUCATION FOR CHILDREN AND THEIR PARENTS MODEL I: A ONE-HOUR SESSION

PURPOSE:

To help children begin to understand and become familiar with the worship service of your congregation.

MATERIALS NEEDED:

1. Name tags and markers

2. Paper and crayons in narthex

3. Copies of "Find the Church" (Worship Resource #1)

4. Learning Centers—materials for centers will vary according to ones chosen for class

PREPARE TO TEACH:

1. One month before the class, get the names and addresses of all the children you plan to include. Send a letter to the children and their parents, telling about the class and inviting them to come. Be clear about where and when the class will be held. Include a copy of "Welcoming Children to Worship" in each letter.

2. Allow at least a week to prepare for the centers. Skills of drawing, printing, and some creating are involved. You may want to look for some helpers for the preparation work.

3. Set up the room you will use so that it is inviting and looks fun! Use lots of color.

4. Be sure that your teaching plan allows at least thirty minutes for the learning centers.

ARRIVAL TIME:

As the children and parents arrive, greet them with a smile and name tags. Show them where they can work on the beginning activity, "Find the Church" (Worship Resource #1).

GROUP TIME:

1. When most of the group has arrived, ask them to join you around the "Sanctuary Game" (Worship Resource #2). Have the children sit on the floor around the game. Parents may sit on the floor or in chairs behind their children. Play the game.

2. Have the children take their seats again. Ask who they think has the most important job during the worship service. Listen to their answers. Then surprise them by saying that it is really the congregation (boys and girls and their families and church friends) that does the most important work of worship. It is easy for us to think of the sanctuary as an auditorium. The pastor, organist, and choir may be seen as the actors and the congregation as the audience. But really, the congregation are the actors, and the pastor, choir, and organist are the players. God is the audience. The songs we sing, the prayers we pray . . . all the things we do in worship are to praise and honor God!

LEARNING CENTERS:

Invite children and parents to explore the learning centers. Be sure that each child has someone to work with him or her, to help with reading and instructions.

CLOSING:

At the end of class time, call everyone together for a closing prayer.

Find the Church

To do this puzzle you will need to look at Psalm 122:1. Find "I" at "START." Draw a line from one word of the verse to the next as you find them on the puzzle. You should have a drawing of a church building when you are finished (From CE:SA *Living the Word,* Level 4, Grades 1–2, Student's Resource Book, Vol. 4. © 1983 Geneva Press).

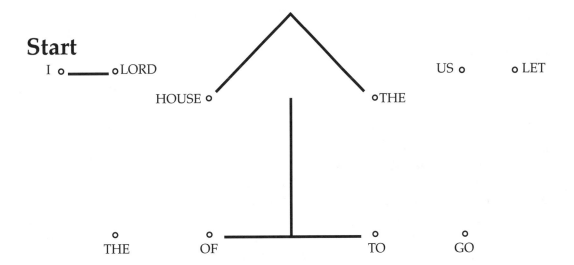

The Sanctuary Game

PURPOSE:

To learn about and better understand the special names and parts of the sanctuary and what happens there in worship.

MATERIALS NEEDED:

1. A permanent-press white sheet of a size that best represents the inside of your sanctuary. With permanent markers (a laundry marker is the least likely to "bleed" onto the fabric), draw a flat outline of your sanctuary with the parts named. Worship Resource #2 is a sample to give you an idea, but you will draw your sanctuary.

2. Pictures of all the parts of your sanctuary—photographs are best. Include: pulpit, organ, communion table, baptismal font, cross, offering plates, choir loft, stained glass windows, pews, hymnbooks, Bibles, communion cup holders, chancel, narthex, candles, etc.

3. Index cards with the pictures mounted on them and the name of the pictured item (these may be laminated). If you think you will have more children than the items pictured, make extra "hymnbook" and "Bible" cards.

INSTRUCTIONS:

See if the children know what is pictured before them. They may need a few clues ("Here is a door where people come in" or "Here is the cross that is on the wall"). Talk about the name for the building where we worship . . . sanctuary. Some sanctuaries are like ours, some are very small, some are very big. What makes a building a sanctuary is that it is a place where people come to worship God. Talk about all the things shown for your sanctuary (pews, narthex, pulpit, choir loft, etc.). Let the children choose one of the cards which has been prepared for the game. If there are more cards than children, give some to the adults. Ask everyone to look at their card and see if they can see that spot on the game. Help those who need it. Review the meanings as you go around. Then ask everyone to take off their shoes and go to the spot indicated on their card. Some of the areas will be crowded, but that's part of the fun.

Ask the children what they like best about worship. Discuss their answers. Ask what they like least. The answer will probably be "the sermon." Talk with the children about why the sermon is hard for them . . . it's a long time to sit still and be quiet . . . they may not understand much of what the pastor is saying. Explain that the sermon is very important because it is the time when the pastor helps us think about the Bible and what God is saying to us. Children need to listen to the parts they can understand. Suggest that they try listening to the sermon long enough to hear one thing they can draw a picture of. Try it at worship and ask the children to take their pictures to the narthex during the last hymn. The pictures can be posted, or the children can hold them for the congregation to see as they leave. Tell the children where they will find paper and crayons in the narthex to use for their "sermon pictures." Even though the sermon seems long, it's important to be quiet so the people around you can listen. Think about some of the things that would be good to do (color, read, count all the blue pieces in stained glass windows, do puzzles in children's bulletin, etc.). Encourage them to participate in the rest of the service and wait till the sermon for their "quiet activities."

Worship Resource #2

SANCTUARY OUTLINE

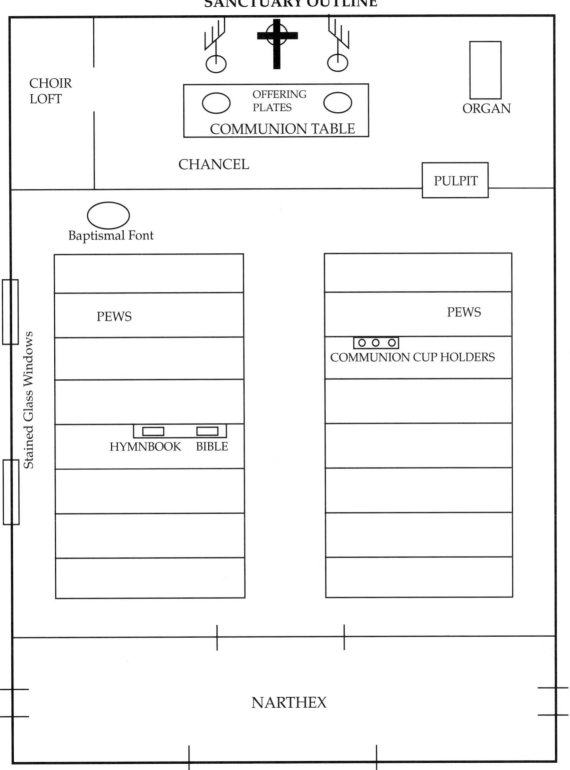

ABOUT LEARNING CENTERS

Now is the time for the children to enjoy the learning centers. The directions you give will depend on the length of the class or how many sessions you will have. If you use "Worship Education Model I," which is to be done in one hour, plan to use thirty minutes of that time on learning centers. Tell the children that you would like them to enjoy each of the centers around the room. If they find one that is their favorite, they may want to go back to it after they have done the others. If you have a longer time or more sessions, the children might have more latitude. Just be prepared for some of them to love to play with the money and others to want to make five hymnbook markers.

You should decide how you want things to move along. For small churches or classes where there is a wide range of ages, you may want to include centers which are geared to older children. These are marked in the book.

Before you begin to make your centers, read "Tips for Using This Book."

Each learning center should be self-directing. The "Student Instructions" are given with each center. These should be copied and mounted on stiff backing or printed on poster board. They should be displayed on an easel or posted on the wall in each center. Parents or older children will need to read these instructions for younger children. The following pages contain the suggested learning centers. You will set these up according to the amount of space and time that is available for the session. Here is a sample room arrangement to give you some ideas as you plan for your own class.

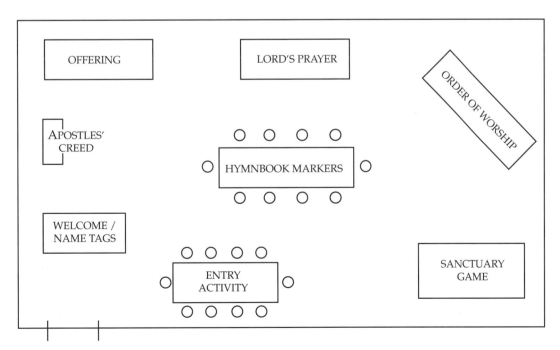

Apostles' Creed Learning Center
(For Older Elementary Children)

PURPOSE:

To let children hear, say, and begin to learn the Apostles' Creed.

MATERIALS NEEDED:

Copies of the Apostles' Creed

A tape recording of someone reading the Apostles' Creed—read once, then repeat it, asking children to say the creed with you

Tape Recorder

Poster with Student Instructions

INSTRUCTIONS:

Have the tape recorder set up so that it is ready to play. Lay copies of the Apostles' Creed nearby so that the children may follow along as it is being read. Have them take the copies home so they may begin to learn it. Some children may not know how to operate a tape recorder and will need some help in rewinding the tape.

STUDENT INSTRUCTIONS:

1. A creed says what one believes. The Apostles' Creed says what the church believes.

2. Push the "PLAY" button on the tape recorder. Look at a copy of the Apostles' Creed as you hear it.

3. After you hear it one time, you will be asked to say it with the reader.

4. When you finish, rewind the tape.

5. Take a copy of the Apostles' Creed home with you and learn it with your family.

The Apostles' Creed

I believe in God the Father Almighty, Maker of heaven and earth,

And in Jesus Christ his only Son our Lord; who was conceived by the Holy Ghost, born of the Virgin Mary, suffered under Pontius Pilate, was crucified, dead, and buried; he descended into hell; the third day he rose again from the dead; he ascended into heaven, and sitteth on the right hand of God the Father Almighty; from thence he shall come to judge the quick and the dead.

I believe in the Holy Ghost; the holy catholic Church; the communion of the saints; the forgiveness of sins; the resurrection of the body; and the life everlasting. Amen.

(Source: *Book of Confessions*, The Constitution of the Presbyterian Church [U.S.A.], Part I, copyright © 1996)

Hymnbook Marker Learning Center

PURPOSE:

To help the children learn how to use the hymnbook by making a bookmark to use in worship.

MATERIALS NEEDED:

Poster board, cut into size indicated, or cardboard with colored paper glued to one side

Washable markers, stickers, 1/8" ribbon in various colors, cut into 12" strips

Hole Punch

Worship Bulletins

Hymnbooks

Poster with Student Instructions

INSTRUCTIONS:

Lay materials out on a table. Make a sample for the children to see.

STUDENT INSTRUCTIONS:

1. Punch three holes at one end of the strip of poster board.

2. Put one end of a ribbon through a hole and tie it around the top of the bookmark. Repeat with the other two holes.

3. Decorate the strip of poster board with markers and stickers. Put your name on it.

4. Take a worship bulletin and hymnbook. Find the hymns and mark them in the hymnbook with your hymnbook marker to learn how to use it.

5. Take your hymnbook marker to worship with you and use it to mark the hymns.

Lord's Prayer Learning Center

PURPOSE:

To help children begin to learn and understand the Lord's Prayer.

ACTIVITY 1:

Materials Needed: Copies of the Lord's Prayer (Worship Resource #4)

Phrases of the Lord's Prayer. These may be cut-up paper copies of Worship Resource #4 or phrases printed on strips of poster or tag board

Copies of the "Lord's Prayer Guide" (Worship Resource #5), for adults working with the children

Poster with Student Instructions

INSTRUCTIONS:

Scatter the phrases on a table or on the floor. Place stack of the Lord's Prayer and "Lord's Prayer Guide" nearby.

STUDENT INSTRUCTIONS:

1. Look at the copy of the Lord's Prayer.

2. Arrange the parts of the prayer in the right order, discussing what each means.

3. Read over the prayer several times so that you begin to learn it.

4. Take copies of the prayer and "Guide" home to learn.

ACTIVITY 2:

You will need:

Copy of "The Lord's Prayer with Motions," (Worship Resource #6)

Someone to lead the group

INSTRUCTIONS:

Have the children do this activity with a partner. Note: If you are using this activity in several sessions, you may want to introduce it at the first session and then repeat it at subsequent sessions (remember, children like movement and activity).

The Lord's Prayer

Our Father, who art in heaven,

hallowed be Thy name.

thy kingdom come.

thy will be done, on earth as it is in heaven.

Give us this day our daily bread;

and forgive us our debts, as we forgive our debtors.

and lead us not into temptation, but deliver us from evil.

For thine is the kingdom, and the power,

and the glory, forever. Amen.

(Source: *Book of Common Worship*, p. 73, Westminster/John Knox Press, 1993)

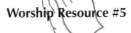

The Lord's Prayer Guide

Work with your child to arrange the phrases of the prayer in order. Let the child do as much as he or she can, but don't hesitate to offer help. As you arrange the phrases together, discuss what each one means. Here are some suggestions for discussion.

1. God is our very special (heavenly) Father because God loves and cares about us always, every minute, every day.

2. God's name is holy and precious. It should only be used in loving ways.

3. God, help us make the earth a loving and happy place, like heaven is.

4. God, we ask you to give us the things we really need. We know other people (farmers, grocers, stores, cooks) help us enjoy the things we need, but they really come, first of all, from you.

5. Please forgive me when I do things that I know are wrong, and help me to forgive other people who are mean to me.

6. God, you are more special and important than anyone in the whole world and you always will be!

Amen. (Yes, that's right!)

THE LORD'S PRAYER WITH MOTIONS

OUR FATHER WHO ART IN HEAVEN, HALLOWED BE THY NAME,

THY KINGDOM COME, THY WILL BE DONE, ON EARTH AS IT IS IN HEAVEN,

GIVE US THIS DAY OUR DAILY BREAD;

AND FORGIVE US OUR DEBTS, AS WE FORGIVE OUR DEBTORS;

AND LEAD US NOT INTO TEMPTATION, BUT DELIVER US FROM EVIL.

FOR THINE IS THE KINGDOM, AND THE POWER, AND THE GLORY, FOREVER. AMEN.

Offering Learning Center

PURPOSE:

To explore what happens to the money from the offering and to better understand how it is used.

MATERIALS NEEDED:

"Play money" (may be purchased at a toy store or borrowed from Monopoly game) in a basket or offering plate

Cards with names and pictures of items that show some of the ways your church's money is used, such as an electric bill, church school curriculum, picture of minister, and other staff people in need, missionaries, etc.

Poster with Student Instructions

INSTRUCTIONS:

Lay the cards out on a table. Put the basket of money near by.

STUDENT INSTRUCTIONS:

1. Part of worship is giving an offering. Pretend that this money is the offering we received today.

2. On the cards look at some of the ways it is used in our church.

3. Decide how YOU would divide the money and put it on these cards.

4. When you are finished, put the money back in the basket.

EXPANDING THE LEARNING CENTER:

List on poster board the names of each of your Session committees. Glue photographs illustrating how each committee spends its money to do God's work. Examples:

Worship Committee—pictures of hymnals, music, candles

Staff Committee—pictures of members of staff

Property Committee—pictures of someone repairing the roof

Order of Worship Learning Center

PURPOSE:

To help children become familiar with the order of worship and begin to understand what it means.

MATERIALS NEEDED:

Either

New shiny (not non-stick) jelly roll pans (cookie sheet with sides) to represent each side of your bulletin

"Order of Worship" strips (Worship Resource #7A, B, C, D) copied on card stock and cut apart

Magnetic tape (available at hardware or craft stores)

Several copies of your Sunday worship bulletin

Poster with Student Instructions

Or

Poster board cut to about twelve inches by eighteen inches, to represent each side of your bulletin

Velcro dots (two for each "Order of Worship" strip), available at fabric stores

"Order of Worship" strips (Worship Resources #7A, B, C, D) copied on card stock and cut apart

Several copies of your Sunday worship bulletin

Poster with Student Instructions

INSTRUCTIONS:

To make the center using the cookie sheets, cut the magnetic tape into one-half inch pieces. Turn the "Order of Worship" strips over and stick a piece of the tape near the ends of each strip. To make the center using poster board and velcro, cut the poster board into the needed sizes. Turn the "Order of Worship" strips over and stick one side of the velcro dots near the ends of each strip. Lay the strips on the poster board to determine where the other side of the velcro dots should be placed in order to match.

STUDENT INSTRUCTIONS:

1. Look at the worship bulletin and at all the different parts.

2. Arrange the strips in the same order as that of the bulletin. The pictures will help you understand each of the parts of worship.

ORDER OF WORSHIP STRIPS

Prelude

Candlelighting

Call to Worship

Hymn

Prayer of Confession

Assurance of Pardon

Worship Resource #7B

ORDER OF WORSHIP STRIPS

Congregational Reading

Pastoral Prayer/Lord's Prayer

Ministry of Music

Scripture Lesson

Sermon

Offering

Worship Resource #7C

ORDER OF WORSHIP STRIPS

Affirmation of Faith

Gloria

Hymn

Children's Sermon

Passing the Peace

Concerns of the Church

Worship Resource #7D

ORDER OF WORSHIP STRIPS

Communion

Baptism

Doxology

Hymn

Benediction

Postlude

Worship Fold-ups Learning Center
(For Older Elementary Children)

PURPOSE:

To help children clarify the role of the pastor, choir, ushers, elders, and the people in worship.

MATERIALS NEEDED:

Copies of the five enclosed sheets (Worship Resources #8A, B, C, D, E). Center the "WHY" on the back of each square. Use a different color paper for each of the five and cut dotted lines to size indicated.

A sample of one of the sheets with the centers folded to the center

Pencils or pens

Poster with Student Instructions

STUDENT INSTRUCTIONS:

1. Take one of the five sheets and fold the four corners of the square into the middle as shown.

2. Read the information on the back of the square. Then turn it over.

3. Lift each corner and write your answer to that question. Answer the WHY question in the middle.

4. Continue with another color until you have done all five Worship Fold-ups.

Back of folded sheet

Front of folded sheet

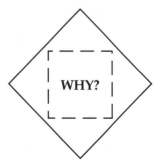

Inside of folded sheet

(Adapted from *Successful Activities for Enriching the Language Arts* by Betty Coody and David Nelson. Waveland Press, Inc.)

Worship Resource #8A

WORSHIP FOLD-UPS *(For older elementary children)*

WHERE?

WHEN?

THE CHOIR

The choir is the group of people who help to lead in worship by singing and helping us to sing. On Sunday morning at worship, the choir sits or stands in the choir loft. They sing special music that they have learned to help us think about God. They sing the hymns and the responses with the congregation to help us know how this music should sound and to praise God along with the other people in the church.

The choir is a very important part of our church at worship.

WHAT?

WHO?

WHY?

Worship Resource #8B

WORSHIP FOLD-UPS *(For older elementary children)*

WHERE?

WHEN?

THE USHERS

The ushers are some of the people who help with worship on Sunday morning. They do many things. They greet us as we come into the sanctuary and help visitors feel at home. They give us a bulletin so that we can know what will be happening in the worship. They help people find a place to sit. They pass the offering plates so that we can give our gifts to God.

The ushers are a very important part of our church at worship.

WHAT?

WHO?

WHY?

Worship Resource #8C

WORSHIP FOLD-UPS *(For older elementary children)*

WHERE?

WHEN?

THE PASTOR

The pastor leads the congregation in worship in the sanctuary on Sunday morning. One of the pastor's most important jobs at worship is preaching the sermon. The sermon helps us think about what God has said to us in the Bible and helps us know what we should do about what God has said.

Usually the pastor preaches the sermon standing in the pulpit. It is good for people in the church to listen to and think about what the pastor says in the sermon.

The pastor is a very important part of our church at worship.

WHAT?

WHO?

WHY?

Worship Resource #8D

WORSHIP FOLD-UPS *(For older elementary children)*

WHERE?

WHEN?

THE PEOPLE

When God's people come to worship we are called "a congregation," which means "those who have come together." On Sunday morning when we come to worship, we see the choir, the pastor, and the ushers helping with the worship. All of them are important, but MOST important to worship is the people! For our job is to worship God! The pastor, choir, and ushers help us do our job of worshiping God.

The word worship comes from two English words from long ago..."worth-ship." So, when we come to worship God, we have come to show what we think God is worth, and to say that we love God and want to be God's people. We show these things to God by our songs, our prayers, our kindness to those around us, our giving, and by learning more about what God would like us to do and be.

Of all those at worship,
the congregation has the most important job!

WHAT?

WHO?

WHY?

Worship Resource #8E

WORSHIP FOLD-UPS *(For older elementary children)*

WHERE?

WHEN?

THE ELDERS

The leaders of our church are elders. They do many things as a part of the worship service. They may lead in the worship, reading the scriptures and leading the prayers. They help at baptisms. They serve Communion. They may preach the sermon. They greet visitors and make them feel welcome. They receive new members into the church.

Elders are a very important part of our church at worship.

WHAT?

WHO?

WHY?

WORSHIP EDUCATION FOR CHILDREN AND THEIR PARENTS MODEL II: FOUR ONE-HOUR SESSIONS

FOCUS GROUP:

Children ages 5, 6, and 7 and their parent(s)

BACKGROUND:

The four sessions that follow are designed to meet the need for a short-term course that involves parents as co-teachers/learners with their children who are pre-readers or young readers. At the end of each session, suggestions will be given to extend the session and include older elementary-age children.

The four sessions deal with: the place of worship,
what worship is,
the plan that helps us worship,
talking with and listening to God.

The purpose of these sessions is to explore the sanctuary and learn about it; begin learning about worship as our response to God; become familiar with the order of worship used by the congregation; and learn prayers, songs, and responses so that participation in worship is possible as the child joins his or her family for corporate worship.

SESSION ONE: WE HAVE A SPECIAL PLACE TO WORSHIP

MAIN IDEA:

We have a special place to gather as families to worship God.

PURPOSE:

To help teach each child to
- (a) experience the sanctuary
- (b) learn names for the furnishings and
- (c) feel comfortable in the place of worship

BIBLE VERSE:

Psalm 122:1

PREPARE TO TEACH:

1. Reflect on Psalm 122 and think of all the ways we can help children and make them feel glad when they hear, "Let us go to the house of the Lord."

2. Consider how the children "see" the sanctuary. Experience it with all the senses as the children will.

3. Make arrangements for the class to tour the sanctuary as part of the session. If scheduling prevents this, consider making a video of a guided trip to the sanctuary, or take slides and make a cassette tape describing the sanctuary. Encourage parents to take their child to the sanctuary when it is empty and explore it together.

4. Invite the pastor and organist to meet the class on the tour if possible.

5. Acquaint yourself with the furnishings, origin of names like baptismal font, theology of the architecture, or any special history of your sanctuary.

MATERIALS NEEDED:

1. Identification tags for each place and item that will be visited in the sanctuary (narthex, pulpit, communion cup holders, etc.). Tags consist of items lettered on four-inch wide poster board and hung by ribbon or cord.

2. Tape of hymns such as "The Church Is One Big Family," "We Are Your Church, O God," "I Am the Church," and "The Doxology."

3. Copies of "Find the Church" puzzle (Worship Resource #1).

4. Make Sanctuary Game. Game board is a large permanent press sheet on which you draw with fabric pen a flat outline of your sanctuary, particularly the chancel area (see Worship Resource #2). Take photographs of each item that is to be pointed out on the tour—narthex, pew, stained glass window, lectern, pulpit, organ, choir loft, communion table, cross, candles, Bible, baptismal font, hymnbook, etc. Mount photos on squares of poster board. On the back of each card, write a question or two. For suggested questions, see Worship Resource #9.

ARRIVAL TIME:

1. Have the cassette tape of selected hymns playing.

2. Greet each child and parent(s). If this is a large group or if people do not know one another, have them make name tags.

3. Invite each child with the assistance of parents to complete the "Find the Church" puzzle (Worship Resource #1) based on Psalm 122:1. Encourage parents to help their child read the completed puzzle.

GROUP TIME:

1. Use Psalm 122:1 to introduce the activities for the session. Show a picture (old teaching picture) of people going to church and talk about the verse.

2. Introduce the word *sanctuary.* You could say something like: "The Bible helps us understand that worship of God can happen any place and almost any time. It is good to have a special place to gather as God's people. It has always been that way. In the Bible we read about the different places/settings that were created for worshiping God. We are part of the people of God and we belong to this family of families called _____ Church. We have a special place to gather for worship and it is called the *sanctuary.*"

3. Prepare for the guided tour of the sanctuary. "We are going to see the sanctuary and _____ will be your guide. (If someone else is serving as a guide introduce them.) There are lots of things in the sanctuary that have special names. (Show identification tags. Give each child a tag to carry.) You will want to listen and use your eyes to discover all the new things that you can. When the tour guide talks about your 'tag' please place it on the item or place."

4. Go on the tour, stopping to point out and talk briefly about each item. Be sure to collect all identification tags before returning to the classroom. An alternative to going to the sanctuary would be to use a video or show slides made in your sanctuary. Play a cassette tape describing it.

5. Debrief from the trip and answer any questions.

6. Play the "Sanctuary Game." Spread the sheet on the floor and invite the children to stand around the edges. Place the mounted photos in a basket. To play the game, the child draws a picture from the basket, looks at it, and identifies it. A non-reader hands the photo card to the leader, who reads the question that is on the back of the card so that the child can answer the question. An older child reads the answer to the question(s). Upon answering the question, the child goes to stand on the sheet where the item is located.

7. Close by repeating Psalm 122:1 and singing one of the hymns.

ADDITIONAL ACTIVITIES FOR OLDER CHILDREN:

1. Have children look up and find places and occasions where God's people worshiped: Genesis 12:8; Exodus 23:8; Exodus 12:21–28; I Kings 6:1–3; Luke 4:16; Luke 6:12, 17; John 6:1–4; Romans 16:5. This could be a worksheet.

2. Have a "Can You Discover???" sheet for the older children to take with them on a clipboard. On the worksheet list objects found in the sanctuary and have the children fill in the location of each item and its use.

WORKSHEET:

CAN YOU DISCOVER???

Object or Place	Location	Use
1. Narthex		
2. Pew(s)		
3. Hymnbook		
etc.		

Suggested Questions for Sanctuary Game (Model II)

PHOTO QUESTIONS

1. *Baptismal Font*

The water for baptism is put here. What is it called? What other word comes to mind when you hear the word "font?" What special event happens around this stand?

2. *Lectern*

What is this stand called? What is usually located on it?

3. *Narthex*

What is the name of this room outside the sanctuary? What do people do in this room?

4. *Communion Table*

What is the name of this table? What special meal is served from this table?

5. *Bible*

What book is this? Where is this big Bible located in the sanctuary?

6. *Pew bookrack*

Each pew has a rack with books. Name them. What are the round holes for?

7. *Organ*

What is this instrument called? Who plays it?

8. *Nave*

This is the main part of the sanctuary. What is it called?

9. *Pews/Chairs*

What are the places called where people sit to worship? Do you know how many pews or rows of chairs are in the nave?

10. *Stained Glass Windows*

Windows made with beautiful colored glass are called_____. Name places where you saw stained glass in our sanctuary.

11. *Cross*

What is this? Who do we remember when we see it? Where is the cross located in the sanctuary?

12. *Chancel Area*

This area of our sanctuary has a name. What is it called?

13. *Pulpit*

Name this important place in the chancel of our church. What does the minister do while standing here?

14. *Candles*

The light of candles reminds us of the one who is the "light of the world." Who is that?

15. *Carvings*

Do you remember seeing this symbol carved in wood? Where is it? Name some other places where you saw carvings.

SESSION TWO: WORSHIP IS OUR RESPONSE TO GOD'S LOVE

MAIN IDEA:

Praise is the heart of worship.

PURPOSE:

To help each child begin to understand that worship is one way we respond to God's love for us. To recognize that praise is the core of worship. To learn the song of praise, the Doxology, that is sung each Sunday in worship.

BIBLE VERSES:

Psalm 100 (TEV) (paraphrased); Psalm 150

PREPARE TO TEACH:

Read and reflect on the two psalms. Why do we come to worship? How will the children begin to understand about praising God? What happens in corporate worship that conveys praise?

MATERIALS NEEDED:

1. PRAISE word cards for the children to use to make rubbings. Cut the poster four inches by length needed. Attach vinyl letters or glue on cut-out letters to spell the word. For older children, other praise words such as alleluia, hallelujah, rejoice, and amen can be used. Prepare newsprint or manila art paper in six-inch strips and gather used crayons for this art activity.

2. Copies of the Doxology (Worship Resource #10) for families to use and take home.

3. Tape of someone playing hymns of praise: "All People That on Earth Do Dwell," "Praise the Lord!" "Praise Ye the Lord," "The Doxology."

4. Pictures (photos or teaching pictures) of people worshiping.

5. Poster of Psalm 100 (TEV). (Worship Resource #11)

6. Copies of your church's worship bulletin.

7. Poster of words of the Doxology (see Learning Activity #3) on large sheets of craft paper, leaving space for children to draw pictures. If time is a problem, use pictures from magazines and old leaflets or curriculum, and let the children pick ones that will illustrate the words, or provide magazines for them to find their own.

ARRIVAL TIME:

1. Greet each family and visit with them.

2. Invite those arriving early to review by playing the Sanctuary Game (from Session 1).

GROUP TIME:

1. Play the Doxology (piano or cassette tape).

2. Use Psalm 100 printed on a chart to talk about what worship is. Ask the children to pick out words in the psalm that tell something that we do in worship. Underline these words as the children call them out. Talk about why we come to worship. Suggest that some clues are found in the psalm. In worship we gather together as a church family to pray, sing, listen to the word of God, read from the Bible, and talk about it. We also give our offering and get ready to go out to serve others. Everyone is to do these things as our response to God's great love shown to us. Show pictures of persons at worship.

3. List some of the reasons we have to praise God. Then ask: "What are some of the ways we praise God?" Read Psalm 150.

4. Music and singing are good ways to praise God. Songs of praise to God are called hymns. One of the hymns we sing each Sunday is called the Doxology. "Doxology" means "giving praise." Give out copies of the Doxology and go over the words. Play it and then sing it together.

LEARNING ACTIVITIES:
(Use Recording of Hymns of Praise to Provide Background Music.)

1. Use the worship bulletin and identify all the times praise is offered in worship.

2. Make a rubbing of the word PRAISE. Tape the PRAISE word card securely to the table. Have the children place a six-inch, pre-cut strip of newsprint or manila paper over the word card and hold firmly in place with one hand. Rub the broad part of a "broken" crayon over the surface to bring up the word PRAISE.

3. Invite children to work in groups of fours to illustrate the Doxology on the pieces of craft paper.

4. Close by letting the groups show their illustrations of the Doxology. Sing the Doxology. Give each child a copy of it to take home. Suggest that families use it as their blessing before meals.

Praise God from whom all

flow.

Praise God all

here below.

Praise God above ye

Praise Father, Son, and Holy Ghost.   Amen.

ADDITIONAL ACTIVITIES FOR OLDER CHILDREN:

Choose from among the praise words (alleluia, hallelujah, rejoice, amen). Do some research on the word chosen. Find a definition of the word in a dictionary. Find at least one place the word appears in the Bible and one hymn where the same word appears. Then make a rubbing of the word.

Worship Resource #10

DOXOLOGY

Praise God, from whom all blessings flow;

Praise God, all creatures here below;

Praise God above, ye heavenly host:

Praise Father, Son, and Holy Ghost.

(Source: *The Presbyterian Hymnal*, Westminster/John Knox Press, 1990, no. 593)

Worship Resource #11

PSALM 100 (paraphrased)

Sing to the Lord, all the World!
    Worship the Lord with joy;
        Come before God with happy songs.

Never forget that the Lord is God.
God made us; and we belong to God;
We are God's people, we are God's flock.

Enter the temple gates with thanksgiving;
Go into its courts with praise.
Give thanks to God and praise God.

The Lord is good;
God's love is eternal
And God's faithfulness lasts forever.

Psalm 100 is taken from *The Good News Bible*, in Today's English Version. © American Bible Society 1966, 1971, 1976. Used by permission.

SESSION THREE: WE HAVE A PLAN TO HELP US WORSHIP

MAIN IDEA:

The bulletin we receive when we enter the sanctuary each Sunday morning guides us through our worship.

PURPOSE:

To help children become familiar with the various parts of worship and to learn what action is appropriate for worshipers and leaders in worship. To begin to understand how to use the worship bulletin.

PREPARE TO TEACH:

Remember that very young readers will find the worship bulletin overwhelming. We can help them identify key words and symbols that are used in worship. (Note: Some congregations print helpful drawings so their young worshipers will know what action each part of worship requires — singing, praying, listening, etc.)

MATERIALS NEEDED:

1. Copies of your worship bulletin.

2. Copies of the hymnal, Bible, and the *Ritual of Friendship* (if your church uses one).

3. Enlargements of the pictures on the "Order of Worship" strips (Worship Resource #7A, B, C, D) until it fills half a page (four inches). Mount each picture on colored construction paper and write on the back a brief explanation of that part of worship for your use in Group Time #3.

4. Copy the "Order of Worship" strips (Worship Resource #7A, B, C, D) and cut apart for use by children in Group Time #3.

5. Place a card for each major division of worship as listed in Group Time #3. If these divisions are not used in your worship bulletin, omit this.

ARRIVAL TIME:

1. Welcome each child and family. Invite the child to draw a picture of their church. If the worship bulletin shows your church, the child could color it.

2. Have the Doxology (cassette tape from Session 2) playing.

GROUP TIME:

1. Bring everyone to a circle of chairs.

2. Introduce the worship bulletin and give each family a copy. Dialogue might include these ideas:

When you go to a baseball or football game you get a program. What are other events you go to that have programs (music events, special community events, etc.)?

The bulletin the usher hands you as you enter the sanctuary is like a program. It lets us know what to do and when to do it. It also lets us know who is leading us in our worship.

This is our plan for worship. It helps us act together. It tells us when to sing, pray, read from the Bible, listen, and give.

Following this plan helps us join in worshiping God together.

3. Invite parents and children to open their copy of the worship bulletin and identify the major divisions of worship:

Assemble in God's name;

Proclaim God's Word;

Give Thanks to God;

Go in God's Name.

Put the placecards—one for each major division of worship—on the floor. Distribute the "Order of Worship" illustrated strips among the children. You will work through the entire worship service using the enlarged picture cards and explanations. Tell the group that as you talk about each part of worship, you want them to 1) find, with the help of their parent or older friend, that part in the worship bulletin and 2) when the picture on their strip matches the one you hold, bring it up and place it on the floor in the correct order. Proceed through the entire worship service.

4. Use the "Order of Worship" strips to make and play these games:

A. "Worship Bingo" (illustrated "Order of Worship" strips can be arranged on poster board to make a "bingo" card).

B. "Who Does What?" Sort the "Order of Worship" strips into categories—Minister, Choir, Elders/Deacons, Congregation, combination of these.

C. "What's the Action?" Sort the "Order of Worship" strips into categories such as Singing, Praying, Listening, Talking, Giving.

D. "Worship Concentration": Have pictures on one set of cards and explanations of each picture on another set of cards. To play, mix up the cards and place each one face down on the table. A player turns up one card and tries to make a match with another one. The player making the most matches wins.

5. Close by reading Psalm 100 from the chart made for use in Session 2.

ADDITIONAL ACTIVITY FOR OLDER CHILDREN:

Use "Worship Fold-ups" (Worship Resources #8A, B, C, D, E).

SESSION FOUR: WE PRAY AS A PART OF OUR WORSHIP

MAIN IDEA:

Praying is talking to God and it is also waiting and listening to learn God's way for us to live.

PURPOSE:

To introduce children to the different kinds of prayers that are part of our worship. To help children begin to learn the Lord's Prayer.

BIBLE VERSES:

Luke 11:1–4 (the Lord's Prayer)

PREPARE TO TEACH:

Read Luke 11:1–4 and reflect on this familiar passage. When did you last ask,
"Lord, teach me to pray"?
What are we praying for when we say, "may your kingdom come"?
What "food" do we need for each day?
How are you at forgiving everyone who does you wrong?
What kinds of "hard testing" are we hoping to avoid?
How do the children we teach hear these petitions?

MATERIALS NEEDED:

1. A poster or bulletin board with the different kinds of prayer we pray in the worship service. See sample bulletin board, Worship Resource #12.

2. Envelopes for each child with the Lord's Prayer (Worship Resource #4) cut into strips (one phrase per strip) and a copy of the "Lord's Prayer Guide" (Worship Resource #5).

3. Puzzles of the Lord's Prayer out of poster board. Print the prayer and then cut it up into a number of puzzle pieces. Find an old teaching picture of Jesus praying, mount it on poster board, and then cut it up into puzzle pieces.

4. Copies of your church's worship bulletin and highlighter pens.

5. Copies of "The Praying Game" (Worship Resource #13). Collect small pictures from old church school curriculum that illustrate each of the five kinds of prayer. Or make copies of "The Lord's Prayer with Motions" (Worship Resource #6) and cut out the pictures (without the words).

6. Recording of "The Lord's Prayer," if available.

ARRIVAL TIME:

1. As children and parents arrive, invite them to sit at tables to play one of the Order of Worship games from Session 3 to review and reinforce what they have learned.

2. While children are still at the tables, give them copies of the worship bulletin and high-lighter pens. Ask each child, with parents' help to underline the word "prayer" or "pray" each time it appears in the bulletin.

GROUP TIME:

1. Ask the children to bring their bulletins and gather for group time, using the recording of "The Lord's Prayer," if desired.

2. Ask children to count how many times they found the words "prayer" or "pray" in the bulletin.

3. Engage children in conversation about what they think prayer is and when they pray. The conversation could include ideas such as:

—Prayer is talking to God. We can do that any time and anywhere.

—Prayer is also waiting and listening to learn God's way for us to live.

—We have a lot to talk with God about, and so we have different kinds of prayer. Find some in your bulletin.

—Use your poster with prayer glove to explain the different kinds of prayers.

"Thank You"	Prayers of Thanksgiving
"I love you, God"	Prayers of Adoration
"I'm sorry, God"	Prayers of Confession
"Show us the way to care for"	Prayers of Intercession
"Please help me"	Prayers of Petition
"I'm Listening, God"	Prayers of Meditation

4. Invite children to return to their tables and play "The Praying Game" (Worship Resource #13). Put the pictures you have collected, or cut out, in a box or basket next to a stack of games. To play the game, students choose a picture to illustrate each kind of prayer.

5. Return to the circle and introduce the prayer that all the people pray together in worship—the Lord's Prayer.

   —Open the Bible and indicate that the words to the prayer were given when the disciples asked Jesus to teach them to pray. Read Luke 11:1–4.

   —Give each table group a puzzle of the Lord's Prayer to assemble. Encourage a parent to read it with the children when the puzzle is done. Have a recording of the Lord's Prayer playing while they work.

6. Close by praying the "Lord's Prayer with Motions"(Worship Resource #6). Give each family an envelope of phrases of the Lord's Prayer (Worship Resource #4) for them to work on at home. Include "The Lord's Prayer Guide" (Worship Resource #5) in the envelope also.

ADDITIONAL ACTIVITIES FOR OLDER CHILDREN:

1. Sing the West Indian folk tune version of the Lord's Prayer (*The Presbyterian Hymnal*, no. 589).

2. Write some prayers of adoration, thanksgiving, petition, confession, intercession, or meditation.

3. Illustrate each phrase of the Lord's Prayer.

Worship Resource #12

PRAYER CHART

CONFESSION

We have not obeyed
God and...

Add pictures.

THANKSGIVING

We thank God for...

Add pictures.

INTERCESSION

We pray for others.

Add pictures.

ADORATION

We love God.

Add pictures to
illustrate kind
of prayer.

PETITION

We ask God for
what we need.

Add pictures.

MEDITATION

We listen to God.

Add pictures.

Adoration

Thanksgiving

Confession

Intercession

Petition

Meditation

Worship Resource #13

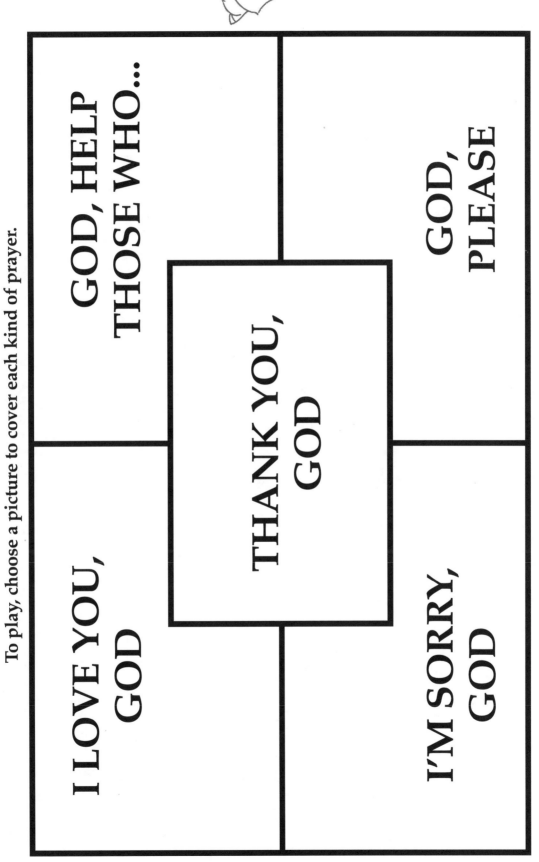

THE PRAYING GAME

To play, choose a picture to cover each kind of prayer.

GOD, HELP THOSE WHO...

GOD, PLEASE

THANK YOU, GOD

I LOVE YOU, GOD

I'M SORRY, GOD

EDUCATIONAL MODELS FOR WORSHIP EDUCATION

There are a number of educational models, printed materials, and resource books to aid both parents and congregations in carrying out their educational responsibilities.

1. *PREM* (Presbyterian Reformed Educational Ministry). Offers two curricula, *Celebrate* and *Bible Discovery*, which include sessions on worship in its age-group materials for church school.

2. *Gateways to Worship* by Carolyn C. Brown. Provides fifty-two sessions for preparing Kindergarten–Grade 2 to learn and experience worship. Abingdon Press, 1991.

3. Logos (Youth Club) curriculum. Offers a course for middle elementary ages: *God's People Worship* by Carolyn Brown. Course 4. Pittsburgh, PA: The Logos Program Associates, 1989.

4. *Young Children and Worship* by Sonja M. Stewart and Jerome Berryman. Offers a model for young children to experience the meaning of the Service for the Lord's Day. The multi-sensory model is based on the Montessori approach to education which Sofia Cavalletti of Italy developed for the Roman Catholic Church. Stewart and Berryman have redesigned her methods to be used in The Reformed Church in America. Westminster/John Knox Press, 1990.

Other denominations provide materials as well:

5. *God's Children in Worship Kit.* A thirteen-session study aimed at systematically teaching children (Kindergarten–Grade 2 and Grades 2–4) and their parents about worship. Nashville: Discipleship Resources (United Methodist Church).

6. *Alleulia!* series. Curriculum to acquaint children with worship and music. Based on the Lectionary: Year A, Year B, and Year C. Minneapolis: Augsburg Publishing House.

7. *Consider the Child* by Patrice Rosner. Forty sessions to be used during the worship hour with children ages three to five. St. Louis: Christian Board of Publication, 1990.

PART 3
SACRAMENTS

THE SACRAMENTS

BAPTISM

> **Session Outline**

> **Ideas for Celebrating a Baptism**

>> Baptism Mixer (Baptism Resource #1)

>> Baptism Bingo (Baptism Resource #2)

>> Baptismal Shell (Baptism Resource #3)

>> The Belonging Game (Baptism Resource #4)

>> Baptismal Symbols Game (Baptism Resource #5)

>> "The Sacrament of Baptism" (Baptism Resource #6)

>> "John, Jesus, and Baptism" (Baptism Resource #7)

COMMUNION

> **Session Outline**

> **Ideas for Making a First Communion a Special Time**

>> Communion Bread (Communion Resource #1)

>> The Remembering Jesus Game (Communion Resources #2A, B, C, D)

>> Certificate of Welcome (Communion Resource #3)

>> Communion Game (Communion Resources #4A, B, C, D, E, F)

>> Communion Stole Pattern (Communion Resource #5)

>> A Teaching Meal (Communion Resource #6)

THE SACRAMENTS

The sacraments (Baptism and Communion) are gifts of God to assure us of God's love. One writer has phrased it this way: Sacraments are "heavenly mysteries." As such we never fully understand them. Each time we participate in them, we unwrap the gift afresh, as Word connects with life experience. So the sacraments are gifts to help us grow in faith and be faithful.

God is the principle actor in each of the sacraments. It is our promise-making and promise-keeping God who has, according to scripture, acted in history on our behalf. This is made unmistakeably clear in the birth, life, death, and resurrection of Jesus Christ. Both sacraments arose from the ministry of Jesus. They focus on the work of Christ and link us to the events of Christ's life, death, and resurrection. The sacraments have to do also with the forgiveness of sins and with God's claiming us as part of God's own people.

While children will not understand the complex theology of the sacraments, they can easily grasp the basic meanings. The materials in this section are designed to help children think about the sacraments and to help the adults who are working with the children as they examine their own beliefs.

Baptism. There are many different ways to understand the Sacrament of Baptism. The concept of baptism as a sign of our belonging to the family of God is the focus of this study. Belonging is vitally important to young children. They feel dependent on the acceptance and approval of the adults in their lives. Understanding that their baptism is an affirmation that they belong to God and are a part of the church, and that making mistakes doesn't change that fact, is very reassuring to children.

Communion. The Sacrament of Communion is presented here as a time to remember Jesus. Remembering is something that young children understand. For those reared in the church, there is already much they can remember about Jesus and his love and care. So the primary focus is on remembering. However, because of the language about sacrifice and blood that are usually a part of the church's celebration of communion, it is also necessary to talk with children about these issues. The concepts you'll find discussed are:

— The grape juice is a symbol of Jesus' blood . . . there will never really be blood in the cups.

— Jesus was killed on the cross because he wouldn't stop showing people God's love, nor would he stop asking them to love others. That love was so powerful — stronger even than death — that it brought Jesus back to life again. When we know Jesus' love, we want to live the way he lived. Jesus promises to give us the gift of life that never ends. Though our bodies die, our spirits live always in heaven with him.

There are always many questions from the children. A few of these can be answered simply, but most of the questions reflect the child's inner grappling with the faith. The best response to this sort of question is, "What do you think?", which allows the child to find his or her own answers.

The games, learning centers, and activities are designed to help children explore their thoughts and feelings about the sacraments. Be prepared for lots of questions to arise out of this exploration. It is important that the adults who work with the children prepare themselves with prayer, with study, and with discussion with other adults, as they prepare to assist a child in his or her own understanding of the sacraments. Remember, *the sacraments are heavenly mysteries*! There are no simple answers, and none of us ever fully understand. So, be a partner with the children as they learn and ponder. *They* frequently turn out to be the teachers!

SACRAMENT OF BAPTISM
(A ONE-HOUR SESSION OUTLINE)

PURPOSE:

To communicate to children and their parents several aspects of the meaning of the Sacrament of Baptism. Meanings of Baptism to be dealt with:

1. We each belong to a family.

2. Baptism is the sign of our belonging to the family of God—the church.

3. The church family is made up of lots of families.

4. We have symbols to remind us of the Sacrament of Baptism.

MATERIALS NEEDED:

1. Manila paper, crayons, or markers.

2. Copies of "Baptism Mixer" (Baptism Resource #1) or "Baptism Bingo" (Baptism Resource #2) for all participants.

3. Copies of the "Belonging Game" (Baptism Resource #4), mounted on poster board. Read "A Word About Making the Games" ("Tips for Using This Book"), page 2.

PREPARE TO TEACH:

1. Arrange with your minister a time to meet your class in the sanctuary. You may also wish to invite the Clerk of Session to bring the church's permanent roll book for children, where names are recorded following baptism.

2. Invite parent(s) to bring either a picture taken at the time of their child's baptism or about the time of the baptism.

ARRIVAL TIME:

Greet each child and parent(s) as they arrive and invite them to play "Baptism Bingo." Share with them that today we are going to be talking about being a part of a family, and also belonging to a church family. Invite each child to draw a picture of their family and encourage them to include all members. (Be sensitive to children who are part of a single-parent family or stepfamilies.)

GROUP TIME:

1. Ask everyone to gather in the circle of chairs and bring the picture they have been working on. Talk about families—there are lots of different kinds of families. Display the children's pictures. Introduce the idea that the church is a family made up of individual families. All of us belong to the family of God.

2. Baptism is the way by which we are welcomed into the church family. Baptism tells us we belong to God and that God loves each one of us. At the time of our baptism, the whole church affirms that we belong and that we are to care for one another and tell others about God's love. Whenever we see someone being baptized, we can remember God's love and care for us and for all people.

3. Prepare to meet the minister in the sanctuary at the baptismal font. Note: When making this arrangement, emphasize the importance of meeting the children at their level of understanding. This will require some special attention to words used in explaining the Sacrament; time for the children to look in the font and touch the water; as well as time to let them ask questions.

Alternatives to a trip to the baptismal font: show a video of an actual baptism with a commentary by the minister to help the children understand, or show a filmstrip from *Celebrate Curriculum Resource Kit for Elementary Grades Year 1* and talk about it.

4. Return to the classroom and, if your church keeps an album of pictures taken at the time of baptism, help the children find their pictures in the album. Be sure to alert families whose children were baptized elsewhere to bring a picture with them to share with their child. Invite parents to share their memories of the child's baptism. Then record the child's baptismal date and full name on a cutout of a shell (Baptism Resource #3) to take home or display.

5. Play the "Belonging Game" (Baptism Resource #4). To make the game, cut along dotted line and glue to the dotted line. Mount on poster board and laminate if desired.

6. Close by singing "I Belong" (sung to "Jesus Loves the Little Children"):

> *I belong for I am baptized*
> *Into God's own family.*
> *"Child of God" is now my name;*
> *And God's promises I claim.*

(To personalize for use at a baptism, see "Ideas for Celebrating a Baptism.")

ADDITIONAL ACTIVITIES:

1. Use "The Sacrament of Baptism" (Baptism Resource #6) as a play.

2. Learn more about Jesus' baptism by using "John, Jesus, and Baptism" (Baptism Resource #7) and create a script for a drama center.

3. Play "Baptismal Symbols Game" (Baptism Resource #5).

4. Make baptismal greeting cards to be sent to infants or children being baptized.

5. Use the symbols on the "Baptismal Symbols Game" (Baptism Resource #5) to create rubbing cards. To do this, enlarge the symbol of the dove, shell, and water on cardstock paper, cut around each symbol, and mount on cardboard. Secure card to table, place paper over the symbol, and have the child use the broad side of a crayon to rub across the symbol.

6. Make mini-banner on clear plastic using permanent marking pens. (The clear plastic could be a sheet of transparency or a piece of clear vinyl, available at hardware or fabric stores.) Suggest that the banner include one of the symbols of baptism, the child's name, and date of baptism. Note: There may be children in the class who have not been baptized. To avoid embarrassment you could say, "That's all right. That is something you have to look forward to."

IDEAS FOR CELEBRATING A BAPTISM

The baptism of a child or infant is always a high point in the life of a congregation. A baptism offers a number of special ways to include children in worship.

1. An elementary-age child may carry in a pitcher of water to be used in the baptism. The pastor meets the child at the baptismal font, receives the pitcher, and then incorporates the pouring of the water into the baptismal service.

2. An elementary-age child may carry in the permanent roll book of the church and present it to the pastor in the chancel. The roll book is then placed on a stand near the baptismal font. Following the baptism, the pastor asks the clerk or the elder who has assisted in the baptism, to enter the child's name. This is a very visible way for the congregation to realize that the child is now a baptized member of the church.

3. Print the names of children participating in the service in the church newsletter and worship bulletin.

4. Speak to the children. As the pastor asks the congregation its vow, a word can be included to the children as to what role they can play in this child's life, such as being a friend, learning their name, or helping them at church.

5. Introduce the baby to the congregation. Many pastors carry the baby into the congregation as a part of the service, speaking about baptism, its meaning, and the church's responsibility to this child. When this is done, the children of the church can see the baby in a way that they may not be able to if the whole service happens in the chancel.

6. Sing a special song. Following the baptism, the family may stand before the congregation with the child while they all affirm what has happened using the following song. Because it is a tune that is familiar and easy for children, they will be able to participate. (Sung to "Jesus Loves the Little Children")

   Hannah (child's name) belongs, for she is baptized,
   Into God's own family.
   Child of God is now her name,
   And God's promise hers to claim,
   For she's baptized into God's own family.

7. Make a special card. As a part of their church school class, children may make cards or a picture to present to the child being baptized.

8. Ask a photographer in the church to be prepared to take pictures after the service. Begin a baptismal picture album for the church.

BAPTISM MIXER

(For older elementary children, youth, and adults)

Find someone who fits the description, can identify the symbol, or answer the question in each square. Ask that person to sign his or her name in the square.

	Someone baptized at Christmas time	Someone who cried when baptized as a baby	What is a sacrament?	
Date of your baptism	What is this object?	Someone baptized in a church other than one currently attending	Someone baptized the same month you were	Someone baptized by a relative (aunt, grandfather, uncle, etc.)
Someone who has been going to the same church since infancy	Someone baptized as a baby	Your full NAME CHILD OF THE COVENANT	Who baptized Jesus?	Someone baptized at Easter time
What kind of baptism is this?	Someone who can name the minister who baptized him or her	Someone baptized as a preschooler	Someone baptized in another denomination	Person baptized in same church as parent
Someone who remembers own baptismal date	Someone baptized as 1st, 2nd or 3rd grader	Why is water used for baptizing people?	Someone baptized as an adult	Someone baptized in church currently attending

BAPTISM BINGO
(For younger children and small groups)

Find someone who fits the description in each square.
Ask that person to sign his or her name in the square.

Someone who was baptized in this church	Someone who knows what this symbol means	Someone who remembers being baptized
Someone who knows what this symbol means	God's ♥ is FREE for ME! _____ Sign your name!	Someone who knows what this symbol means
Someone who is an elder and has helped with a baptism	Someone who knows who baptized Jesus	Someone whose child was baptized in this church

BAPTISMAL SHELL

Baptism Resource #4A

The Belonging Game

WHO BAPTIZED JESUS?

MOVE AHEAD 1 SPACE.

Jesus commanded his followers to go make disciples and baptize them and teach them. (Matthew 28:19)

YOU are learning more about God's love every day.

GIVE A CHEER!

Being a part of God's family means we are called to care for others.

NAME 1 WAY YOU CAN CARE FOR OTHERS.

Jesus was baptized.

Read about it in the Bible. Matthew 3:13–17.

Often the child is brought out into the congregation as a way of saying "Meet our new family member."

REMEMBER the words the minister says when baptizing a person: "I baptize you in the name of the _____ _____ and _____."

ROLL A DIE TO PLAY

You belong to a family.

NAME YOUR FAMILY. Move ahead 1 space.

God planned for us to be part of a bigger family—the CHURCH

NAME YOUR CHURCH.

Baptism Resource #4B

The Belonging Game

ALWAYS REMEMBER YOUR BAPTISM

Move ahead of 1 space.

MAKE A CROSS ON YOUR FOREHEAD WITH YOUR FINGER AND SAY

I AM A CHILD OF GOD

I AM BAPTIZED

The whole church family also promises to share the Good News and help the child learn and grow.

YOU ARE LOVED!!!

Parents promise to put their trust in Christ and to teach their child about God's love. What are these promises called?

MOVE AHEAD 1 SPACE.

Name the people who stand around the baptismal font for the sacrament.

PRACTICE saying BAPTISMAL FONT by repeating it 3 times NOW.

Where is the water kept for Baptism?

WHAT IS IT CALLED?

NAME ONE REASON WATER IS IMPORTANT

Every Sunday the church family comes together to worship.

ASK THE PLAYER JUST BEHIND YOU TO JOIN YOU IN THIS SPACE.

Two special acts are part of our celebration of worship. One is COMMUNION. YOU NAME THE OTHER SPECIAL ACT.

Move ahead 2 spaces.

BAPTISM is the special way of saying, "You belong to God's family the church."

Say Amen!

What does the minister sprinkle on a person's head during the Sacrament of Baptism?

BAPTISMAL SYMBOLS GAME
Find the symbol that matches the description in each box and put it in the box.

SHELL	WATER	DOVE
Some churches use a shell to pour the water during baptism. The three drops of water with the shell remind us that we are baptized in the name of the Father, Son, and Holy Spirit.	All life depends on water, so God chose water as the special sign of baptism.	At Jesus' baptism, God sent a dove from Heaven. The dove was a sign of God's promise to be with Jesus always and to help him do God's work. When we are baptized, God gives us that same promise.
BELIEVER BAPTISM	**JESUS' BAPTISM**	**BAPTISM OF INFANTS**
People who were not baptized as children are baptized when they come to join the church as youth or adults.	Jesus was baptized in the Jordan River by John. His baptism showed everyone that Jesus was ready to serve God.	Believing parents may bring their children for baptism. Both the parents and the congregation make promises to teach the child about Jesus' love.

Baptism Resource #5B

BAPTISMAL SYMBOLS GAME

Copy and cut apart and give each child a set of six different pictures (two sets included)
to use with the Baptismal Symbols Game.

The Sacrament of Baptism

Some people are baptized when they are babies. The whole congregation takes part. Here are words you might hear at a baptism.

Minister: "In Jesus Christ, God has joined us together in the family of faith which is the church."

Minister (speaking to parents): "Do you intend your child to be Jesus Christ's disciple, to obey his word, and show his love?"

Parents: "We do."

Elder (speaking to the people): "Our Lord Jesus Christ ordered us to teach those who are baptized. Do you, the people of the church, promise to tell this child the good news of the gospel, to help him or her know all that Christ commands, and, by your fellowship, to strengthen her or his family ties with the household of God?"

People: "We do."

Minister: "Let us pray. Almighty God, as we baptize with water, baptize us with the Holy Spirit."

Minister and People: "O God, who called us from death to life, we give ourselves to you, and, with the church through the ages, we thank you for your saving love in Jesus Christ our Lord. Amen."

Minister: "(Name of child), I baptize you in the name of the Father, and of the Son, and of the Holy Spirit. Amen."

Reprinted from *Learning at Church*, Year 1, Grades 3–4, *Celebrate Curriculum*. © 1988 Presbyterian Publishing House.

John, Jesus, and Baptism

People had never met anyone like John the Baptist. He didn't seem to care much what he ate or what he wore. All that mattered to him was giving God's message to the people. Crowds followed John. They heard his voice thunder, "You are Abraham's children, but you must turn from your sinful ways. Get ready. Repent. The kingdom of God is coming."

The people listened carefully. They knew John was right. "What shall we do?" they asked.

"Come and be baptized to show you have changed," John urged.

Many people thought John might be the Messiah. So John said clearly, " I am not the One you are waiting for, but he is coming."

One day, when John was baptizing at the Jordan River, Jesus came and stood in the crowd. He told John, "Baptize me." John did not understand. "This is what God wants," said Jesus. So John baptized Jesus there.

Immediately afterward, as Jesus prayed, God's Spirit came down on him as a dove, and a Voice said, "You are my much loved Son. I am well pleased with you."

No other baptism was ever like this. What did the dove and the Voice mean? These two unusual events showed Jesus that he was doing what God wanted him to do.

Why did Jesus come to be baptized?

Beginnings are important. Jesus' baptism marked the beginning of his work for God. Jesus' baptism was a way of showing everyone that the Messiah was now with them.

John had called the people to get ready for the Messiah. They had repented. Now they were ready to listen and learn. They felt a need for God. Jesus began after this to teach them about the kingdom of God.

Reprinted from *The Readabout,* Year 1, Grades 3–4, *Celebrate Curriculum.* 1988 Presbyterian Publishing House.

*PREM MATERIALS ON BAPTISM

CELEBRATE and *BIBLE DISCOVERY*

The Presbyterian Church (U.S.A.) provides many excellent teaching and learning materials on the sacraments. Dated pieces for *Celebrate*, such as students' leaflets, are not listed, because they may be ordered only for the quarter for which they are intended for use. Teachers' books, teaching kits, and resource books are reusable. Young children's curricula are recycled every two years, and elementary materials are recycled every three years.

Bible Discovery contains materials on the sacraments, but they are dated and are ordered only for the quarter in which they are used, and are not available for reorder at a later time. However, some of them may be found in presbytery and synod resource centers.

AGES 3 - 4

Celebrate, Year 1, *Leader's Guide*	
Bible Background for Teachers	pp. 9–10
Unit 2, Session 3	pp. 26–28
Bible Background for Teachers	pp. 58–59
Unit 6, Session 3	pp. 72–74
Celebrate, Year 2, *Leader's Guide*	
Bible Background for Teachers	pp. 9–10
Unit 1, Session 1	pp. 12–15
Unit 1, Session 2	pp. 15–17
Unit 1, Session 3	pp. 17–20

AGES 4 - 5

Celebrate, Year 1, *Teacher's Guide*	
Bible Background for Teachers	pp. 23–24
Unit 1, Session 3	pp. 35–36
Unit 1, Session 5a	pp. 39–40
Celebrate, Year 1, Storybook: *The Christ Church Troupers*	
"Being Baptized"	pp. 14–19
Celebrate, Year 2, *Teacher's Guide*	
Bible Background for Teachers	pp. 25–26
Unit 1, Session 3	pp. 36–38

GRADES 1 - 2

Celebrate, Year 1, *Teacher's Guide*	
Unit 5, Session 2a	pp. 87–88
Unit 5, Session 2b	pp. 89–90
Celebrate, Year 1, *Learning at Church*	
"Symbols of Baptism"	p. 92
"The Sacrament of Baptism"	p. 93
Celebrate, Year 3, *Teacher's Guide*	

Covenant People curriculum resources replace PREM in the year 2000. However, PREM materials will continue to be available in presbytery resource centers and congregational curriculum libraries.

Bible Background for Teachers   pp. 60–62
Bible Discovery, Winter 1988–89 & Winter 1991–92, *Teacher's Guide*
Unit II, Session 2   pp. 32–34
Bible Discovery, Winter 1988–89 & Winter 1991–92, *Bible Storybook*
"A Way to Prepare"   pp. 13–15
Bible Discovery, Year 2, Winter 1989–90, *Teacher's Guide*
Unit II, Session 1   pp. 32–34

GRADES 3 - 4

Celebrate, Year 1, *Teacher's Guide*
Unit 5, Session 2   pp. 70–72
Celebrate, Year 1, *Elementary Teaching Kit*
"When I Was Baptized" Booklet
Celebrate, Year 1, *The Readabout*
"John, Jesus, and Baptism"   p. 52
Celebrate, Year 2, *Teacher's Guide*
Unit 3, Session 4, No. 5   p. 43
Celebrate, Year 2, *The Readabout*
"Baptism"   p. 7
"A Service for Infant Baptism"   pp. 7–8
Celebrate, Year 3, *Teacher's Guide*
Bible Background for Teachers   pp. 49–52
Unit 6, Session 1   pp. 66–68
Celebrate, Year 3, *Elementary Teaching Kit*
Poster on Baptism

GRADES 5 - 6

Celebrate, Year 1, *Teacher's Guide*
Unit 5, Session 2   pp. 67–68
Celebrate, Year 1, *The Sourcebook*
"Baptism"   p. 21
"Baptismal Vows"   p. 21
Celebrate, Year 2, *Teacher's Guide*
Unit 4, Session 1   pp. 67–69
Celebrate, Year 3, *Teacher's Guide*
Bible Background for Teachers   pp. 53–54
Unit 5, Session 2   pp. 72–73
Celebrate, Year 3, *The Sourcebook*
"About Baptism"   p. 38
"Tam's Baptism"   p. 60

SACRAMENT OF COMMUNION
(A ONE-HOUR SESSION OUTLINE)

PURPOSE:

To communicate to children and their parents several aspects of the Lord's Table and to establish a climate for ongoing dialogue on the subject.

MATERIALS NEEDED:

1. A loaf of bread, a bottle of grape juice or wine (whichever your church uses for Communion), a Communion tray, Communion cups, a cloth for the table.

2. Pictures of events in the life of Jesus to post around the room.

3. Words to the song, "We Remember" (see Group Time #2, p. 102) on a large sheet of paper or black board—or make copies to distribute.

4. Copies of Communion Bread "To Use at Home" recipe (Communion Resource #1) and small foil pans (5 3/4" × 3 1/4" × 2"), if you plan to do this.

PREPARE TO TEACH:

1. Confirm that all children involved have been baptized. If they have not, talk to the parents about the fact that our church welcomes baptized children to the Lord's Table. Offer an instructional session about baptism for them and for their child. If they choose, the child may be baptized before the day of Communion. If they choose not to have the child baptized, discuss the advisability of the child's participation in the preparation for the Lord's Table. It is important that their child understand the decisions that are being made.

2. Plan with your pastor and Session to have this instruction class for children who are to be welcomed to the Lord's Table and for their parents.

3. Confirm the date of the Communion when the children will be welcomed.

4. Send letters of invitation and explanation to children and parents, telling the time, place, and purpose of your class.

5. Let the Worship Committee know if you would like for the children to provide the Communion bread and ask if the children may scatter the leftover bread for the birds and take the used cups (if plastic) to be recycled.

6. Reserve time in the sanctuary for use during the class if possible.

7. Call several of the families who will participate. Ask the child to bring something from home that makes them think of someone special when they look at it (a gift Dad brought from a trip, or a book from a grandparent).

8. Set up a table, covered with a cloth. Behind it and out of sight, put a Communion tray, some cups, a bottle of grape juice or wine, and a loaf of bread.

ARRIVAL TIME:

As families arrive, welcome them with a name tag and invite them to look at the pictures of Jesus around the room and see how many of the stories they can remember.

GROUP TIME:

1. Ask the children and parents to gather close and sit comfortably near the table. One by one, invite the children who have brought something to share to tell about his or her object. Help them to share who they remember when they look at the object.

2. Sing together the song, "We Remember."

"We Remember" (sung to "Jesus Loves Me")

Jesus said, "Remember me, When the bread and wine you see."
At his table come and share, Jesus' love and precious care.
Lord, we remember. Lord, we remember. Lord, we remember.
Yes, we remember you.

3. Go over to the table. Tell the group that you want to show them something. Set the tray of Communion cups and a loaf of bread on the table. Explain that when we come to worship and see these things on the table, we remember Jesus. We think of Jesus because this is a special meal that Jesus asked his friends to eat to remember him. Ask the children if the pictures around the room have helped them remember some things about Jesus. Let them share. Mention that during Communion worship, children might like to draw pictures of things they remember about Jesus.

4. Thinking together: At Communion you will hear the pastor talk about Jesus' body and blood. That's because we are remembering that Jesus gave up his life, his body, and his blood, when he died on the cross. The symbols we use are a loaf of bread for Jesus' body and juice (or wine) for Jesus' blood.

Invite the children to join you around a table containing the bread and the tray of filled Communion cups. Hold up the bread and say something like, "Jesus and his friends shared bread the last time they ate together. He told us to share bread with each other when we remember him. Without a knife, how can we share this bread? (Let the children answer.) One way is to break it. (Break the bread.) So when we hear the minister say, 'the bread is Jesus' body broken for us,' we know that at Communion some of Jesus' goodness and power becomes part of us when we eat the bread that is being broken and shared." (Pass the bread around for the children to share.) Show the children the bottle of grape juice (or wine) and explain that this is what will be in the cups at your church when you take Communion. Say something like, "The minister may say, 'This is the blood of Christ.' Is it a trick? At your church or any other church, there will *never* really be blood in the cups. The juice is a symbol to help us remember Jesus. You all know that blood is a symbol for life. What happens if a person has an accident and loses all of his or her blood? (Let the children answer.) To be alive, we have to have blood. The wine is a symbol for Jesus' life. So when we drink the grape juice or wine, we remember Jesus and some of Jesus' life becomes a part of us." (Give juice to the children.)

By now, some of the children may be playing with their Communion cups. Explain that these cups are the special dishes for a very special meal of your church family. If they play with the cups during worship, people around them may be worried that they don't understand about Communion. Say something like, "If you went to your grandmother's house for Thanksgiving and ate off her special plates, what do you think your family would say if you licked the plate or played with it when the turkey was all eaten? Well, that's how it is at Communion. If you play with the cups, you may get some unhappy looks from people around you. So, a good thing to do is to put the cup in the cup holder in the pew as soon as you drink the juice. Then, when church is over, you may take it home and play with it."

5. **Plan for baking the bread:** If you have planned for the children to bake the bread for Communion, return to the circle to talk about it now. You may use the recipe for unleavened bread (Communion Resource #1) and bake the bread as a group. You will need to set the time and place for that and be sure parents understand the plans. If you plan for them to bake the bread at home, give each child two small foil loaf pans and a copy of the recipe (Communion Resource #1) to which you have added instructions about when and where they will bring the bread. The recipe will make one loaf to bring to church for communion and one loaf to enjoy at home.

6. **Move to the sanctuary.** If possible, move the class to the sanctuary. If the sanctuary is not available, continue where you are meeting. Gather around the Communion table. Look at the table . . . feel it, talk about any symbols that are on it. Turn and see what the sanctuary looks like from the table. Discuss who will be there when we take Communion . . . the church, our church family. "Who are some of those people? (Let them name some of the people.) The times when we eat this meal together are very special for our church family, because Communion joins us together with each other, with Jesus, and with other Christians."

7. **Look at the cross** (lead the children in thinking and talking about these ideas). If there is a cross in your sanctuary, sit near it. Ask everyone to look at the cross. Let there be a few moments of silence. Then say, "Does anyone know why we have a cross in our sanctuary? Because Jesus was killed on a cross. The real cross that Jesus died on was not a pretty one like the one we have. It was the place where Jesus was killed because

he wouldn't stop showing people God's love and asking them to love others in the same way.

They killed Jesus' body by nailing him on the cross. There was a lot of blood, and it hurt Jesus very much. His friends and his family cried and cried. When Jesus died, the 'bad guys' thought they had won! They had stopped Jesus from telling and showing people about God's love. But God had a very big surprise for everybody. On the cross Jesus had been having a fight with death, **and Jesus won**! His body died, but his spirit was alive forever. So, when we belong to Jesus, we don't have to worry about what happens when we die. Because, even though it's 'yukky' to think about what happened to Jesus' body and his blood on the cross, it was Jesus' way of giving us a wonderful gift . . . the gift of living forever in heaven with him.

8. **Close by asking everyone to join** in a circle around the table. Lead a prayer, thanking God for Jesus, for his love, and for Communion—our special time to remember Jesus.

ADDITIONAL ACTIVITIES:

1. Bake the unleavened Communion bread together. (Communion Resource #1)

2. Play "The Remembering Jesus Game" (Communion Resources #2A, B, C, D).

3. Play "The Communion Game" (Communion Resources #4A, B, C, D, E, F).

4. Make a cloth for the Communion table and/or stoles for worship leaders. Cloth: Cut fabric to size desired (cover the entire table or make a runner for the table). Decorate with handprints, clusters of grapes, crosses, hearts—stenciled, drawn with permanent markers, felt appliques, or painted with fabric paint. Stoles: Use pattern and instructions (Communion Resource #5).

IDEAS FOR MAKING A FIRST COMMUNION A SPECIAL TIME

Welcoming children to the Lord's Table is still a new thought for many Presbyterians. When parents, Sessions, and congregations see that the children have been prepared and are thinking seriously about Communion, they can enter into the celebration with glad hearts. Here are some suggestions that can help make the day when the children are welcomed a very special day:

1. Invite the children to **bake the bread for Communion**. You may choose to do this as a group at the church or in someone's home. In that case, you will want to use the unleavened bread recipe (Communion Resource #1). Or you might give the children a recipe to make at home with their families (Communion Resource #1). This recipe makes two small loaves of bread. One can be used at home as a part of the family's celebration of the day, and the other brought to church to use for Communion.

2. *Have the children present the bread for Communion.* Whether they have baked it or not, the children who are being welcomed to the Lord's Table may process during the opening hymn holding the bread to be used for Communion. They may present it to the pastor at the table and then return to the congregation to sit with their families.

3. *Be sure that the names of the children being welcomed to the table are printed in the church newsletter and worship bulletin.* You might want to include a brief explanation of the preparation the children have received.

4. *Invite the children and their parents to meet with the Session.* On or near the Sunday of the children's welcome, ask the Session to call a short meeting (perhaps on Sunday morning) to meet with the children and officially welcome them. The pastor, educator, or whoever has been working with the children will want to present them to the Session with a few words of explanation about their preparation. The pastor or clerk might ask the children to stand if they are ready to be welcomed at the Table of the Lord. A word can be spoken to the parents, as this is an important moment for them in the keeping of their baptismal vows for their child. A short prayer thanking God for these children should be offered. Then the clerk might present certificates to the children.

5. *Present the children with a certificate marking the event.* Make copies of the enclosed certificate (Communion Resource #3) on a good grade of paper. Have someone with a pleasing handwriting fill in the certificates to present to the children.

6. *Plan for an evening "teaching meal"* (Communion Resource #6) with the children, parents, and elders.

7. *Give the children a small gift* to commemorate the day. Small wooden crosses on a cord can be ordered for a minimal cost or found at many religious bookstores.

8. *Encourage the families to make this a special day for their child.* Grandparents might be invited to visit, a family party or a trip to the child's favorite restaurant might be planned.

COMMUNION BREAD (to bake with the children as a group)

1/3 cup shortening (packed well)

1 cup sugar

1/2 cup milk

1 egg

3 cups flour

2 teaspoons baking powder

1/2 teaspoon salt

Mix first four ingredients, then add dry ingredients, as in cookie baking. Divide into five parts. Roll out each part and put on a greased, floured baking sheet. Score lightly (1/2-inch squares will yield about 80 pieces). Bake at 350° F. for 8-10 minutes. Cool and break apart.

This recipe comes from Maude Alter, a 94-year-old member of First Presbyterian Church, Bryan, Texas. She began to bake the Communion bread for the church in 1974, when the congregation kept complaining about the commercially prepared bread that was being used. Mrs. Alter was given the recipe by a friend from Franklin Street Methodist Church in Johnstown, Pennsylvania.

COMMUNION BREAD (for children to bake at home)

1 cup milk, scalded (do not boil)

1/4 cup sugar

1/4 cup oleo, butter or shortening

1 teaspoon salt

1 package dry yeast

1/4 cup very warm tap water (120-130° F.)

3 1/2 cups unsifted flour (not packed)

1 egg beaten

Add sugar, butter, and salt to milk and stir to mix and melt butter. Pour into a large bowl and let cool to room temperature. Mix yeast with very warm water until all lumps are dissolved. Add 1 cup of the flour to the milk mixture and stir well. Add yeast and stir. Add egg, and then the rest of the flour. Knead on well-floured surface until smooth and elastic (about 5 minutes). Divide dough into half and shape into smooth-topped rectangles. Place into greased pans. Brush tops with melted butter, cover with waxed paper (not tightly). Refrigerate overnight. Bake bread at 375° F. for 25 minutes until golden brown. Note: If bread gets brown before 25 minutes, lay a piece of aluminum foil over it for the remaining time. Bread is done when it sounds hollow when thumped.

Adapted by Cathy Broun from a recipe in *Presbyterian Potpourri*, First Presbyterian Church, Houston, Texas.

Communion Resource #2A

Luke 3:21–22

Luke 2:41–51

Matthew 2:1–12

Luke 2:1–6

START

Communion Resource # 2B

THE REMEMBERING JESUS GAME

1. Trim overlap from game pages. Assemble on colored poster board and laminate if desired. Use a brad to attach an arrow to the numbered circle.

2. Read "Tips for Using This Book: A Word About Making Games," for more ideas.

Luke 18:15–17

Luke 10:38–42

John 6:5–13

The Reme

Luke 11:1–4

Matthew 4:18–22

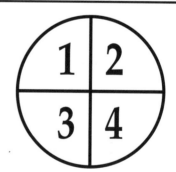

Luke 18:35–43

Luke 15:3–7

Luke 19:35–38

mbering Jesus Game

John 13:1–9

Luke 22:14–20

John 19:23–30

Luke 22:39–44

Communion Resource #2D

John 19:16–22

DIRECTIONS FOR PLAYING THE GAME

1. Put your playing piece on START.
2. Use the spinner or die to move ahead.
3. Tell what you remember about each story of Jesus that you land on.

Luke 24:1–8

Matthew 28:1–7

Say Alleluia!
and go tell others
the Good News.

Communion Resource #3

Certificate of Welcome

PRESBYTERIAN CHURCH (U.S.A.)

This is to certify that

was welcomed to the Lord's Table

on this _____ day of _____ year _____.

at _____ in _____
(Name of Church)   (City/State)

_____   _____
Teacher   Pastor   Clerk of Session

Communion Resource #4A

COMMUNION GAME

TO ASSEMBLE:
1. Make copies of Communion Resources 4A, B, C, D, E.
2. Cut out the instructions and circles.
3. Glue the pieces onto a sheet of poster board, as shown on this page. Draw the tracks that connect the circles.
4. Cut out and glue Directions for Playing in this space on the poster board.
5. Laminate, for longer use.

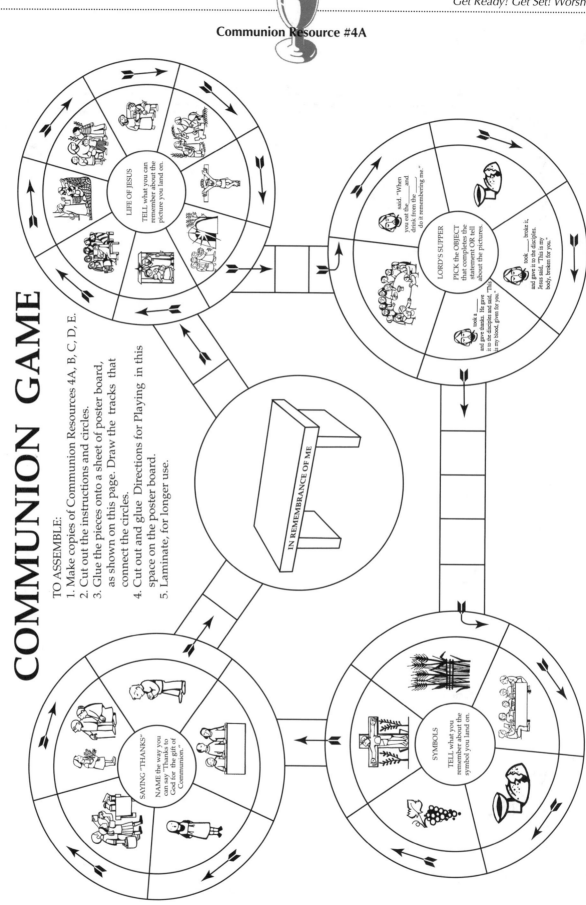

LIFE OF JESUS
TELL what you can remember about the picture you land on.

LORD'S SUPPER
PICK the OBJECT that completes the statement OR tell about the pictures.

said. "When you eat the _____ and drink from the _____ do it remembering me."

took _____ broke it, and gave it to the disciples. Jesus said, "This is my body, broken for you."

took a _____ and gave thanks. He gave it to the disciples and said, "This is my blood, given for you."

IN REMEMBRANCE OF ME

SAYING "THANKS"
NAME the way you can say "Thanks to God for the gift of Communion."

SYMBOLS
TELL what you remember about the symbol you land on.

COMMUNION GAME

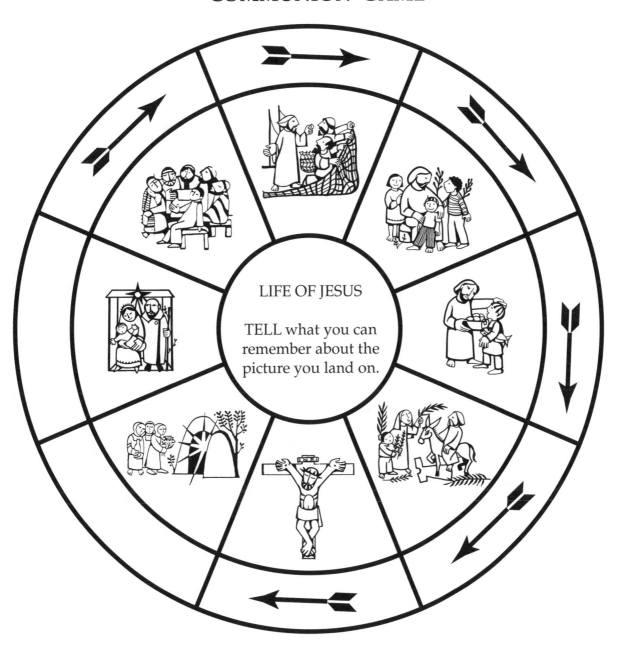

LIFE OF JESUS

TELL what you can remember about the picture you land on.

Communion Resource #4C

COMMUNION GAME

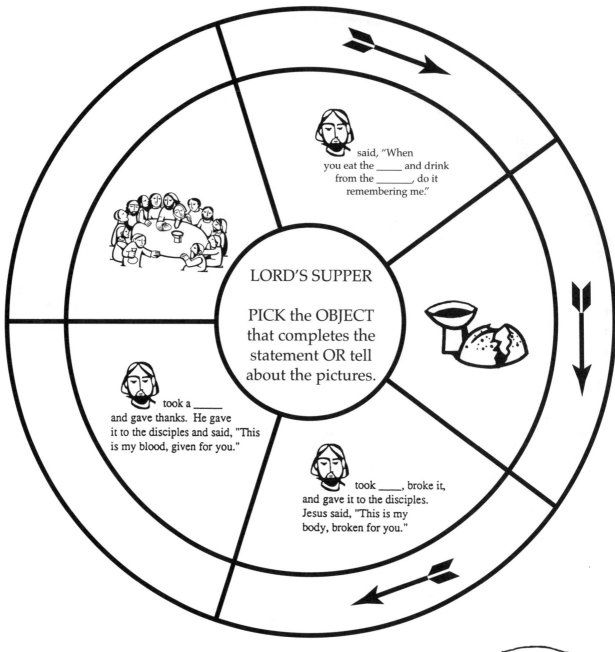

LORD'S SUPPER

PICK the OBJECT that completes the statement OR tell about the pictures.

said, "When you eat the _____ and drink from the _____, do it remembering me."

_____ took a _____ and gave thanks. He gave it to the disciples and said, "This is my blood, given for you."

_____ took _____, broke it, and gave it to the disciples. Jesus said, "This is my body, broken for you."

Make several chalices and loaves of bread for game pieces to use in this circle. Make paper copies or use Shrink Art (*Church Year Idea*, p. 141) from these patterns.

COMMUNION GAME

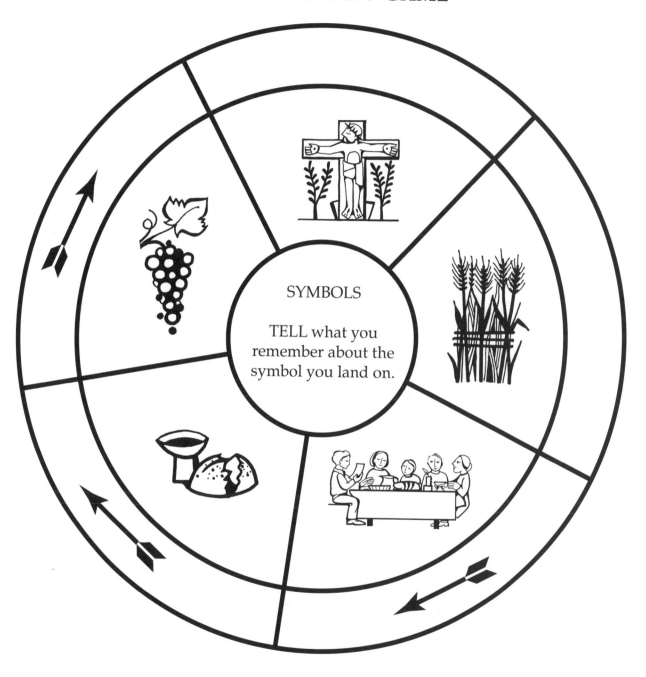

SYMBOLS

TELL what you remember about the symbol you land on.

Communion Resource #4E

COMMUNION GAME

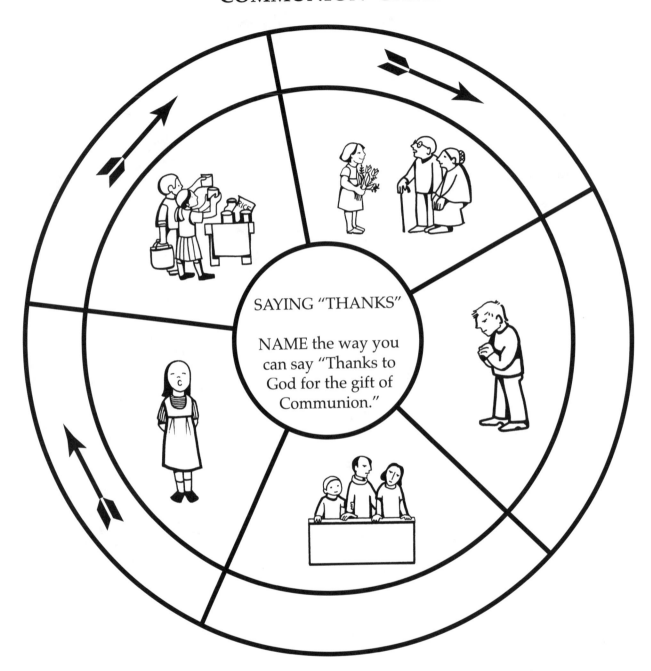

SAYING "THANKS"

NAME the way you can say "Thanks to God for the gift of Communion."

Communion Resource #4F

COMMUNION GAME

Directions for Playing:

1. Begin at the Communion Table and move in the direction indicated by the arrow.
2. Use a spinner to determine spaces to move.
3. Follow the directions given in the center of each circle.

PATTERN FOR PULPIT STOLE

Communion Resource #5

PLACE ON FOLD

Pattern is drawn to use
with paper, felt, or pellon.
(Add 1/4 seam allowance
if you decide to stitch it.)

EXTEND HERE TO DESIRED LENGTH

Communion Resource #6

A TEACHING MEAL

The "teaching meal" is a special meal for parents, their children, and "elder friends" which serves as a conclusion to the Communion preparation study. It is held during the week prior to the welcoming children to the Lord's Table.

The teaching meal is:

the opportunity to experience a memorable meal as a part of preparing for "first" Communion;

an experience of interfacing children, parents, elders of the church, and minister(s);

a unique church meal, in that it is guided by the "elder friend" to provide opportunities to talk with the children about the sacrament and its meanings for them;

the time for a walk-through explanation by the pastor of the celebration (institution) of Communion.

The design calls for an elder to host (hostess) two families, lead the informal conversation during the meal, follow up with the two families, and take part in introducing the children to the Session at its called meeting (see "Ideas for Making First Communion a Special Time") prior to the church's celebration of the Sacrament. Effort is made to make the meal a memorable one with table cloths, candles, flowers, and place cards. If possible, the lights are lowered and the candles lit. The menu might consist of chicken legs, cheese in bite-size pieces, nuts, raisins, apple slices, bread, and juice, plus a vegetable each family brings to share.

Outline of the Teaching Meal:

1. Elder and families meet each other at church the evening of the meal.

2. Pastor or other designated presider shares brief words of explanation about the meal and the fact that the table conversation will be guided by the host/hostess elder.

3. The elder leads families into the hall to the table and offers a prayer of thanks prior to beginning the meal.

4. Guidance for the table conversation:

   a. Invite everyone to look at the food on the table and talk about why they think these foods were chosen. (Jesus might have eaten things like bread, cheese, nuts, raisins, fruit.)

   b. Pass the food and enjoy.

   c. Ask families to share their memories of special meals.
   Questions like these can assist elders in this discussion:
   Where was the meal?
   Who was present?
   What did you eat?
   Why was it special? Or what made it special?
   What else do you remember about the meal?

   d. Next, move the conversation to focus on this meal:
   How is this meal like an ordinary meal?
   How is it different?
   What other times have you eaten these foods?
   When you look back on this meal, what are you going to remember about it?

e. Shift the conversation to the Lord's Supper.
The Lord's Supper/Communion is a special meal for the church family and you have been studying about it.
Provide each child with a set of the pictures printed below. These show events in the last week of Jesus' earthly life. You may talk briefly about each picture as a way to review and/or invite the child to put the pictures in the order of their happening.

f. Elders use their own judgment as to the benefit of inviting adults to reminisce about a special time of celebrating the Lord's Supper.

5. With the meal and guided conversation complete, the pastor or presider invites families to walk with their elder to the sanctuary and find seats in the front rows of pews (or chairs).

The pastor explains about the parts of the Communion service (invitation to the Table, words of institution, prayer to consecrate the elements, distributions of the bread and wine, pattern of serving). In addition, explain about what is appropriate use of the quiet time while the bread and wine are distributed.

If your church plans to have a called Session meeting to welcome children, this is the time to give families the details of that brief meeting.

6. The pastor will close the evening with prayer. One way to do this is to invite everyone to gather in the chancel area around the Communion table, hold hands and close with prayer and sing the "Doxology."

(The idea for this teaching meal came from Thomas G. Long.)

*PREM MATERIALS ON COMMUNION

CELEBRATE and *BIBLE DISCOVERY*

Our denomination provides many excellent teaching and learning materials on the sacraments. Dated pieces for *Celebrate*, such as students' leaflets, are not listed because they may be ordered only for the quarter for which they are intended for use. Teachers' books, teaching kits, and resource books are reusable. Young children's curricula are recycled every two years, and elementary material is recycled every three years.

Bible Discovery contains materials on the sacraments, but they are dated and are ordered only for the quarter in which they are used and are not available for reorder at a later time. However, some of them may be found in presbytery and synod resource centers.

Ages 3-4

Celebrate, Year 1, *Leader's Guide*
Bible Background for Teachers — pp. 9–10
Unit 2, Session 1 — pp.22–24
Unit 2, Session 2 — pp. 24–26

Celebrate, Year 2, *Leader's Guide*
Bible Background for Teachers — pp. 9–10
Unit 2, Session 1 — pp. 21–24
Unit 2, Session 2 — pp. 24–26
Unit 2, Session 3 — pp. 26–29
Unit 2, Session 4 — pp. 29–31
Unit 2, Session 5 — pp. 32–34

Ages 4-5

Celebrate, Year 1, *Teacher's Guide*
Bible Background for Teachers — pp. 23–24
Unit 1, Session 4 — pp. 37–38
Unit 1, Session 5b — pp. 42–43

Celebrate, Year 1, Storybook: *The Christ Church Troupers*
"A Special Meal" — pp. 20–25

Celebrate, Year 2, *Teacher's Guide*
Bible Background for Teachers — pp. 25–26
Unit 1, Session 4 — pp. 38–40
Unit 1, Session 5 — pp. 40–42

Bible Discovery, Summer 1989 & Summer 1991, *Teacher's Guide*
Unit III, Session 3 — pp. 57–60
"God's People Celebrate...in Scripture and Sacrament"

* *Covenant People* will replace PREM resources in the year 2000. However, PREM materials will continue to be available in presbytery resource centers and congregational curriculum libraries.

Grades 1-2

Celebrate, Year 1, *Teacher's Guide*
    Unit 2, Session 1b — pp. 40–41
    Unit 2, Session 1c — pp. 41–43

Celebrate, Year 1, *Learning at Church*
    "The Last Supper" — p. 94
    "The Sacrament of Holy Communion" — p. 95
    "The Last Supper" — p. 103

Celebrate, Year 2, *Learning at Church*
    "The Last Supper" — pp. 18–19

Celebrate, Year 2, *Teacher's Guide*
    Unit 2, Session 1 — pp. 39–42

Bible Discovery, Spring 1989 & Spring 1992, *Teacher's Guide*
    "The Last Supper" — pp. 16–18

Bible Discovery, Spring 1989 & Spring 1992, *Bible Storybook*
    "The Last Supper" — pp. 5–7

Bible Discovery, Spring 1990, *Teacher's Guide*
    Unit II, Session 2   "A Special Meal" — pp. 32–34

Grades 3-4

Celebrate, Year 2, *Teacher's Guide*
    Unit 8, Session 3, No.2 — p. 110

Celebrate, Year 2, *The Readabout*
    "About Communion" — p. 10

Celebrate, Year 3, *Teacher's Guide*
    Unit 1, Session 4 — pp. 24–25

Celebrate, Year 3, *The Readabout*
    "A Change for Communion" — pp. 91–92

Bible Discovery, Spring 1992, *Teacher's Guide*
    Unit I, Session 3 — pp. 16–18
    "Jesus Celebrates with Some Friends"

Bible Discovery, Spring 1992, *Bible Storybook*
    "Jesus Celebrates with Some Friends" — pp. 5–7

Grades 5-6

Celebrate, Year 2, *Teacher's Guide*
    Unit 10, Session 6 — pp. 166–169

Bible Discovery, Spring 1990, *Teacher's Guide*
    Unit III, Session 3

PART 4
CHILDREN IN WORSHIP

**WAYS TO INVOLVE CHILDREN IN
CONGREGATIONAL WORSHIP**

CHILDREN'S MOMENTS
> Books to Use for Children's Moments

WORSHIP AIDS AND CHILDREN'S BULLETINS
> Epiphany Maze (Children's Resource #1)

WAYS TO INVOLVE CHILDREN IN CONGREGATIONAL WORSHIP

Our *Book of Order* (W-3.3201) states:

"In setting an order for worship on the Lord's Day, the pastor with the concurrence of the session shall provide opportunity for the people from youngest to oldest to participate in a worthy offering of praise to God and for them to hear and to respond to God's Word."

In spite of this mandate, not all congregations are actively seeking ways to include children in meaningful participation in worship. Pastors, worship committees, and congregations must all be involved if children are to be included. Utilize the four-session adult study found in Part 1. By the end of Session 4 "Making Plans," you will be ready with recommendations for more effectively involving children and youth. Both the Session and congregation must be informed of new plans and the reasons for them before they are implemented.

Many congregations are already structuring worship in ways that witness to their affirmation that worship is the work of *all* the people of God.

Children/youth as lay leaders in worship can:

sing in choirs;
play hand-bells or hand-chimes;
carry in the Bible;
carry in the permanent record book at the time of baptism;
bring in the pitcher of water for baptism;
read prayers written by a child and/or class;
light candles; serve as greeters or ushers;
participate in special processionals at Advent, Palm Sunday, Pentecost, and Scout Sunday;
participate in the lighting of the candles of the Advent wreath;
design a bulletin cover for a special service.

Ways that enhance the worship service for children:

Select hymns (perhaps one per service) that are particularly suitable for children/youth.
Provide children's bulletins and worship packets.
Welcome baptized children to the Lord's Table for their first time.
Bake and present the bread (Communion Resource #1) for Communion.
Use banner, paraments, stoles (Communion Resource #5), table cloth made by
    children/youth.

Include children's moments in worship service.

Print a suggestion for children to "look for" during worship (How many colors are in today's banner? How many crosses do you see in the sanctuary?, etc.).

Things that enrich children's understanding of worship and the sacraments:

Help set up for worship (hang the paraments, prepare the table for Communion, etc.).

Invite children to scatter leftover Communion bread for the birds and deposit disposable Communion cups for recycling.

Provide intentional age-appropriate instruction about worship for both children and parents (see Worship Education, Part 2).

CHILDREN'S MOMENTS

A time in the service designed especially for children can be one way of including younger members in worship. The time for children must be an integral part of the worship, not just a catchy story or object lesson thrown in to give the children a chance to move around. A children's moment is a good thing when it is crafted to meet the developmental needs of young children. Some of the needs:

1. to have concepts presented in ways that are concrete and that connect with the life experience of young children

2. to allow children to learn in sensory ways (tasting, touching, seeing, etc.)

3. to let children know that they are included in the family of the church

The person presenting the children's moment should resist the temptation to use the children as "straight men" or to capitalize on the cute things that they may say or do. Such things are done at the children's expense, and they interfere with the integrity of worship. Children need to know that they are loved and safe in the family of the church. They need to be free to respond or ask questions without being laughed at.

PREPARATION:

Just as with every other part of the service, serious preparation time is required for a children's time. The presenter need not necessarily be the pastor. It should be someone who is skilled in, or at least willing to learn about, communicating with the children, and who has a knowledge of their developmental characteristics. Language used and approaches chosen must be appropriate. Since young children do not think in abstract terms, "object lessons" are likely to be ignored or misunderstood. Here are some suggested concepts for children's moments:

1. to interpret the scripture for the day

2. to discuss a part of the church year or the worship service

3. to deal with a pertinent event in the lives of the children, the congregation, the community, or the world

Examples of these concepts are found later in this section.

DISCIPLINE:

Plan ahead for how discipline will be handled. It is disruptive and embarrassing to have to correct a child verbally. If the choir sits nearby, enlist several members to quietly and lovingly move to any "trouble spots," should the need arise. Or ask an adult who sits near the front of the sanctuary to be alert to move up. An adult presence is usually all that is needed.

HOW LONG?

Determine the average age of the children who will participate, and plan with them in mind. A good rule of thumb is that children have about a minute of attention span for each year of life. So, if you are preparing for five-year-olds, plan for about five minutes.

QUESTIONS:

Two-way conversations with children can be wonderful but are not an appropriate format for worship. Children do not understand rhetorical or "leading" questions. If you ask a child a question, such as "Do you want to hear a story this morning?", they assume you want an answer. Since the time is short and the children may be embarrassed if they answer inappropriately, it is best to use a format other than questions in children's moments.

WHO AND WHERE?

Plan to present the children's moment in a place where the children can sit down and face the presenter and not the congregation. The presenter should sit in a small chair or on the floor, to be as close to the children's level as possible. An open invitation should be issued to all children to participate. Young children crave the feeling that they "belong," so most of them relish a chance to come forward and be with the group. By about fourth grade, many children choose not to be "singled out," so they may begin to stay with their families. But, it is important to let each child make the decision.

SUMMARY:

Traditions and styles for children's moments differ greatly. What is important is that, if such a time is included in the service of worship, it is done in ways appropriate for young children.

EXAMPLES OF CHILDREN'S MOMENTS:

The following are some examples of children's moments in the subject categories suggested above.

1. Interpret the scripture for the day.
Scripture passage: 1 Peter 3:8–12
Note: For this children's moment you will need several index cards with phrases printed on them. Some of the phrases might be: "I'm sorry," "That hurt my feelings," and "What can we do?"

What to say: "Today we are thinking about some verses in the Bible that help us know what we should do when others are unkind or unfair to us. Most of us know what we usually do when someone is mean to us. Sometimes the words we use are like these: 'You big dummy! I hate you!! You're so stupid!' We say those words because we've heard other people say them. They are a part of the language we use to show we are really angry.

I went to see a friend of mine the other day, and her house looked really funny. There were little signs on everything . . . the window, the table, the door . . . everything! She told me she was learning to speak Spanish. She said it was very hard to learn a new language, one that's different from what she had always spoken. So, she put all those little signs with the Spanish names on things to help her remember.

That made me think that maybe there is a way we could learn a new language to use when we are angry. Our Bible verses today tell us that God would like that very much. So, I've put some words of this new language on cards to remind me to learn them. Here's one that says, 'That hurt my feelings.' This is a good one to use, because it tells the other person why you are feeling angry and bad. Here's one that says, 'I'm sorry.' It's good to use when we make a mistake. This card says 'What can we do?' That question helps us look for new ways to settle an argument.

I'm going to put these cards on my refrigerator door, so that I'll see them every day. When you get home, maybe you and your family could talk about some words in this new language that might work at your house. Remember—it's not easy to learn a new language. You'll have to work hard to learn those new words and to use them. But it's important to do it, for God wants us to speak to each other with love.

Let's have a prayer together. Dear God, we know you want us to speak the language of peace and love to each other, but it's very hard to learn. Bless us as we try to speak to others in a way that will make you smile. In Jesus' name we pray."

2. **Discuss a season or special day in the church year.**
   Note: Epiphany is celebrated on the Sunday nearest the 12th day after Christmas. It is the day when we celebrate the coming of the wise men to Bethlehem to see Jesus. In preparation for this children's moment, purchase "glow–in–the–dark" stars with adhesive backing. These may be found at a teacher supply or an educational toy store. Make copies of the maze (Children's Resource #1). Cut apart sheets of stars. Do not remove the backing. With a glue stick, attach a star to the picture at the beginning of the maze. This way the children do not have to deal with a small loose star.

   What to say: "Today we are celebrating a special day in our church. It is called Epiphany. On Epiphany, we remember the wise men who came from far away to see the baby Jesus. You remember that on the night Jesus was born, lots of things happened. The shepherds, who were just outside the town of Bethlehem, saw angels who told them about the new baby. They went to see Jesus right away. But very far away, some wise men saw a special star in the sky. It was the star that showed them that a new king had been born. Even though they hurried, it took them a long time to get to Bethlehem. Jesus was not a newborn baby lying in a manger when the wise men came. The Bible tells us in Matthew 2:11 that Jesus was a little child and that he and his family were living in a house.

   All the long way from their homes to Bethlehem, the wise men followed the star. They didn't have a map and didn't know where to go. They trusted God to guide them, and that's just what God did!

I have brought something for each of you today, and I'll give it to you before you leave. It's a maze that lets you follow the star and help the wise men find Jesus. But, more than that, the star on this puzzle glows in the dark. When you get home, talk with your family about where you could put this star in your room. Maybe you will want to put it right over your bed, so that when the lights are turned out, you can still see it shining.

I hope this star will remind you that God wants to lead and guide you. God's love is always near us, just like it was with the wise men.

Let's have a prayer together. Dear God, thank you for being with the wise men so long ago and showing them the way to Jesus. Thank you for being with us every day and every night and for giving us your love and helping us to find our way. In the name of Jesus we pray."

3. Discuss a part of the worship service.

Note: This children's moment was done on a Communion Sunday and its purpose was to inform the children that Communion is taken to shut-ins and people in nursing homes each Monday following a Communion Sunday. The kit the pastor uses to serve Communion away from the church was used. Greet the children and call their attention to the Lord's Table that is ready for today's service.

What to say: "I brought something very special to show you today. (Open the kit and let the children see the contents.) It is a little kit that has everything needed in it so that the elders can take Communion to people who belong to this church, but cannot be here with us for Sunday worship. Some of these people are in the hospital, and some of them have to stay at home all the time because they are too sick to go anywhere. Our church does not want these people to feel left out, just because they cannot be here. We think it is important that everyone take Communion and have the opportunity to hear the words that Jesus said to his friends when he gave them the bread and wine at his last supper with them.

So tomorrow our pastor and these elders (call out their names) will come to the church, put juice and bread in the Communion kit, and take it to (list the names of the people who will be visited the next day). They will tell these people that we wish they could be right here with us on Sunday mornings, but since they cannot, we are bringing Communion to them so that they remember they are always part of God's family.

Let's have a prayer together. Dear God, please bless these members of our church family who can't be here for worship today. As they receive Communion tomorrow, help them to know your love and ours. In Jesus' name we pray."

4. Deal with a pertinent event in the world.

Example: In January, 1991, children were very aware of the Persian Gulf War (Desert Storm). Many of them had family members involved, and all of them were seeing it on television and hearing it discussed. On the Sunday following the beginning of the war, a "Hugg-A-Planet" was used in the children's moment. These soft, stuffed globes may be found at many educational toy stores.

The leader said: "This week something very scary has happened in our world. It's called a war. Lots of children and moms and dads are in danger, and some terrible things may happen to our earth. So, this morning, I brought my "Hugg-A-Planet", because this is a good day to give our earth a hug and to remember how much God loves all of the people on the earth.

I'm going to pass the planet around and you can give it a hug, if you want to. Then pass it to someone else. While we do that, we're going to sing a song to remind us that, especially in this scary time, God is taking care of us, of all the people we love, and of the people everywhere.

The song we're going to sing is 'He's Got the Whole World in His Hands' and I'll tell you what each verse is. (The planet was passed as everybody sang.)

> *He's got the whole world in his hands,*
>
> *He's got Saudi Arabia in his hands,*
>
> *He's got all the soldiers in his hands,*
>
> *He's got President Bush in his hands,*
>
> *He's got Saddam Hussein in his hands,*
>
> *He's got all the people in his hands,*
>
> *He's got the whole world in his hands.*

Let's have a prayer together. Dear God, we are feeling really scared and worried today. We are worried about what will happen in the war, and we are worried about the people we love who are soldiers. Please give us peace in our hearts today and peace in our world very soon. In Jesus' name we pray."

5. **Deal with a pertinent event in the lives of the children.**

What to say: "Tomorrow is the first day of school for most of you, and I know that you're feeling really excited, but also a little bit scared. The reason I know is that everyone has those feelings about starting school each year . . . especially if it's a new school.

Your mom or dad can't stay with you at school. Sometimes, your best friend isn't in your class. The teacher and the room and the books are all new. So, it's not surprising that the first day of school is scary!

This morning, I want to teach you a special kind of prayer called a 'breath prayer.' You can pray this prayer with your eyes open. You can say the words in your head instead of out loud. All you have to do is to think about your breathing. Let's stop and do that right now. Think about your breath and breathe it in (demonstrate, pause) and then let out (demonstrate).

Practice a few more times. Now, as you take in your breath, think. 'God is here.' And as you let out your breath, think, "I'm not afraid." Now practice that. I'll say the words while you think them. (Practice: 'God is here. I'm not afraid.') Tomorrow, or any time that you start feeling afraid, use your breath prayer to help you remember that God is with you.

Now let's have a prayer together. Dear God, I pray for all the boys and girls and teenagers of our church as they get ready for another year of school. They have so many important things to decide and to learn. Please help them to remember that you are with them at school, just as when they are at church. Help the scary feeling in their stomachs not to be so bad tomorrow. Thank you for loving and caring for us always. In Jesus' name we pray."

6. Deal with an event in the life of the church, such as the installation of elders.
Note: For this children's moment take a list of Session committees and choose an object to represent the work of each committee. For example, we had a hammer for the property committee, a candle for the worship committee, a telephone for the congregational care committee, a piece of curriculum and a Bible for the education committee, a sack of food for the outreach committee, and a photograph of the church staff for the personnel committee.

What to say: "Today is a special day for our church family, because this is the day we are going to install elders to lead us in doing God's work. Some of these people are already elders. Some will be elders for the first time, so they will be 'ordained,' or called to do God's work. These people will be working very hard for three years with a group we call the Session.

Let me show you some of what the elders do. (Take the toy telephone and pretend to talk into it.) If you are on the congregational care committee you might do this, 'Hello, we just heard that you are in the hospital. Well, the people of the church care about you, so we are going to come visit you today.' (Continue to take the other objects and tell briefly what part of the church's work they represent.)

During worship today these new elders will promise that they will do their best to lead us in our job of doing God's work for God's people. We will pray for them so that they make wise decisions and can help everyone of us find our special gift for doing the work of the church.

Let's have a prayer together. Dear God, thank you for these new elders. Give them strength and lots of patience and love as they serve our church. In Jesus' name we pray."

7. Deal with a special event in the life of the church—installation of new pastor, educator, organist, or other staff.
Note: For this children's moment you will need to have an installation manual for an appliance (in this case, a dishwasher) to use with the children.

What to say: "We got a new dishwasher at our house recently, and this book came with it. It tells exactly how to install a new dishwasher, and it says that if you do not install it correctly, the dishwasher might not work—you won't have any clean dishes!

This afternoon we are going to install our new pastor. So, I brought the *Book of Order*, which tells how a pastor is to be installed in a church. This afternoon, at the installation, the pastor will be making these promises (read a summary of the vows the pastor will take). Then we, all of us, will make some promises, too. (Summarize the vows in language the children can understand.) If the new pastor is present, you can say the pastor's name and nod toward the pastor as you say, 'and this is what we will be promising to you' to the pastor.

One way you can help our new pastor is to teach her your name, and the names of your friends in church. When I was new at this church, you made me feel welcome every time you told me your name, or pointed out other people and told me who they were. The sooner the pastor knows people's names, the sooner she will feel like part of our church family.

Let's have prayer together. Dear God, please bless our new pastor today. Thank you for calling her to serve with us in our church. Help us to think of lots of ways to make her feel welcome, so that she will know that we are glad she has come. In Jesus' name we pray."

BOOKS TO USE FOR CHILDREN'S MOMENTS

1. To interpret scripture:
The Oldest Story in the World by Sekiya Miyoshi. Judson Press (Genesis 1).
The Tiny Sheep by Bunshu Iguchi. Judson Press (Matt. 18:12).

2. To deal with special days in the church:
I Sing a Song of the Saints of God by Lesbia Scott. Morehouse Publishing (All Saints' Sunday).

3. To deal with special events in the life of the children:
A Surprise for Mrs. Dodds by Kathy Long. Augsburg Fortress (Living with older people or difficult people).
Ann Elizabeth Signs with Love by Annetta E. Dellinger. Concordia ("Jesus Loves Me" in sign language).
Love You Forever by Robert Munsch. Firefly Books (Mother's Day or God's love).
The Hating Book by Charlotte Zolotow. Harper Trophy (Being angry with a friend).
What Happened When Grandma Died by Peggy Barker. Concordia (Death).

WORSHIP AIDS AND CHILDREN'S BULLETINS

A number of congregations are endeavoring to assist and nurture young worshipers through the use of "Guides to Worship." The format varies, but usually the guide includes a brief interpretation and illustration of each part of the order of service. Frequently these booklets are placed in the rack along with the hymnal and Bible and actually help worshipers of all ages to understand the integrity of worship.

Children's bulletins are created by other churches on a monthly basis. The children of the congregation are invited to draw pictures for the cover. The other pages are used to interpret a church season or emphasis such as Advent, stewardship, or the Sacraments; or the summary of a series of sermons such as the Ten Commandments or the Apostles' Creed.

Other churches provide worship packets with materials for children to use during worship. The packets may include bookmarks of different colors for marking the hymns and Bible selections for the day; a children's bulletin or workbook on the worship service; pencil, paper, colored markers or crayons, coloring pages, or stickers. These may be put into a drawstring sack or a packet of some kind. Or you may simply make paper and crayons available in the narthex for children to pick up. Whatever is being provided should be in the narthex and marked with a sign. Ushers should be asked to remember to offer these materials to children who are visiting.

There are a number of commercially-prepared bulletins that are based on the Common Lectionary. The scripture passages for the day are explored by the children by way of a variety of puzzles, pictures, and questions. Sources of these bulletins are listed below.

Resources for Creating Children's Bulletins:
Children's Bulletin Idea Book by Faye Fredricks, Nellie deVries and Annetta Dellinger. Grand Rapids, Michigan 49516. Baker Book House, 1987.

Forbid Them Not, Involving Children in Sunday Worship Based on the Common Lectionary, Year C by Carolyn C. Brown. Nashville: Abingdon Press, 1991.

Sources for Purchasing Children's Bulletins:
Children's Worship Activity Sheets, Lectionary-based for every Sunday of the year. For children ages 6-10. Nashville: Abingdon Press.

Gospel Grams, Sunday Activities for Children. Lima, Ohio: C.S.S. Publishing Company.

Children's Worship Activity Bulletins. Based on seasonal themes and the interdenominational three-year lectionary. For children ages 3-12. St. Louis, Missouri: Concordia Publishing House.

EPIPHANY MAZE

PART 5
THE CHURCH YEAR

THE CHURCH YEAR

THE CHURCH YEAR

The church year is a calendar for worshiping God and for learning the story of our faith. This calendar provides a structure in which the church tells the story of faith year after year. The church, like every family, has special times or days that it celebrates. The celebrations center around the events in the life of Jesus Christ and his people. And the church has seasons in which to get ready for these celebrations. The church year is made up of six seasons and fourteen major festival days. The six seasons are Advent, Christmas, Lent, Easter, Pentecost, and Ordinary Time. Each season and day helps the community of faith to look back and to look ahead, to remember and to hope. In this way our faith story is experienced.

The Church Year

IDEAS FOR CELEBRATING THE CHURCH YEAR: There are many ways to help children understand, experience, and celebrate the church year. Here are a few suggestions:

1. Set up a game similar to musical chairs. On the back of each chair, put the name of one of the seasons (put them in the right order) or a teaching picture that relates to the season. Play a recording you have made of someone singing "The Church Year Song." Rather than removing chairs to play the game, designate a "hot seat" by tying a red ribbon on a different chair each time. Whoever sits in that chair will tell something about the season it represents.

   > *"The Church Year Song" (sung to "Twinkle, Twinkle, Little Star")*
   > *Ad-vent, Christ-mas, E-piph-an-y,*
   > *Lent, Ea-ster, Pen-te-cost;*
   > *Every year we celebrate;*
   > *Special stories of our faith;*
   > *Learning how we can believe;*
   > *And God's promises receive.*

2. Use chalk to draw the "Church Year Hopscotch" game (Church Year Resource #1) on a sidewalk or in a hallway.

3. Decorate with seasonal wreaths (Church Year Resource #2).

Advent

The year of the church calendar begins with the celebration of the season of Advent. It begins four Sundays before Christmas and ends at midnight on Christmas Eve. It is a time of actively waiting and getting ready for Christmas. It is the season to remember God's promise and its fulfillment in Jesus' birth, and to hope for Jesus' return and the coming of God's kingdom.

IDEAS FOR CELEBRATING ADVENT   Celebrate Advent with a Posada. "La Posada" is a tradition from Mexico that reenacts the search by Mary and Joseph for a place to stay in Bethlehem. Choose an area of the church where your group can process from a "gathering spot," past several doors, ending up in a large room where a manger (with baby) has been set up. Station a teen or adult behind each door that will be used. Dress two children as Mary and Joseph. They will be leading the procession and knocking on the doors. Before you begin, teach everyone this song to the tune of "Jingle Bells":

> *"Will you help?*
> *Will you help?*
> *We've come from far away.*
> *Our baby will be born tonight.*
> *We need a place to stay."*

Explain to the group that they are there to help Mary and Joseph look for a place for Jesus to be born. With Mary and Joseph in the lead, move to the first door. The children knock and are answered gruffly from inside with a, "What do you want?" The group sings the request for lodging, but are refused. Repeat the process at each door to be used, ending up at the room where the manger is. As the song is sung here, the innkeeper offers the stable and opens the door. (Candlelight will give the room a very special glow.) With Mary and Joseph still in the lead, the group gathers around the manger to sing "Away in a Manger" and have a prayer. Follow with a time of more carols, hot chocolate, and cookies.

Christmas

The season of Christmas begins with Christmas Day and continues for twelve days until the Saturday before the feast of the Baptism of Jesus. The church celebrates the childhood and early adult years of Jesus.

IDEAS FOR CELEBRATING CHRISTMAS   A cake for Jesus. In advance, bake a cake with three tier-layers. During the church school hour, ice and assemble the cake. Around the bottom layer, put twenty birthday candles. On the top, put an angel and a star (in icing or using figures). The candles represent the twenty centuries since Christ's birth. The angel and star represent the messengers God used to tell people of Jesus' birth. The children may host a party for Jesus during the fellowship hour.

Epiphany

The festival of Epiphany falls on January 6th. Sometimes it is called Twelfth Day/Night. The word "Epiphany" means "showing forth." It refers to Christ's being shown to the Magi. The focus is on Christ as the light to the Gentiles. Epiphany, in many churches, includes celebrating the visit of the Magi, the Baptism of Jesus, and the first miracle of Jesus at Cana.

IDEAS FOR CELEBRATING EPIPHANY   Ask a child to lead the processional carrying a glittery star hanging from a pole. As a part of the children's moment, the children may distribute star-shaped sugar cookies to the congregation.

Lent

The season of Lent begins with Ash Wednesday and includes Palm Sunday, Maundy Thursday, and Good Friday. The forty days of this season are for remembering and reflecting on the mystery of Jesus' life and death so that the resurrection becomes ever more meaningful and powerful.

IDEAS FOR CELEBRATING LENT   Purchase a "Shrink Art," "Shrink It," or "Reduce Art" at a craft store (Michael's, Lee Ward's, American Handicraft, etc.). Follow the directions to trace a cross onto the plastic, remembering that the design you draw will shrink to about sixty percent of the original size. Color the crosses or print words. Follow the directions for the type of markers to use. *With a hole punch, make a hole at the top of the cross before baking!* Bake in a regular oven or a toaster oven. Remove and let cool. Let the children add their ribbon or yarn, and they have a special cross to wear during Lent.

Easter

Eastertide includes Easter Day and begins eight weeks of celebrating Jesus' resurrection. Ascension Day (fortieth day after the resurrection) is included in Eastertide.

IDEAS FOR CELEBRATING EASTER   For each child, take a 4"x6" index card, lap 4" ends and tape, making a tube. Use a 12-inch square of pastel tissue paper and two 8-inch pieces of ribbon or yarn. You will need butterfly-shaped crackers, such as Pepperidge Farm Butter Thins. Roll the tissue paper around the tube and tie one end with ribbon. Put some butterfly crackers into the tube, and tie the other end with ribbon. You may want to include a strip of paper that says something like "Easter Means New Life," or "Jesus is Alive." You will, of course, use this activity with the concept of a butterfly hatching out of a cocoon to a new kind of life and the parallel concept of Jesus' resurrection from the tomb. There are many wonderful butterfly pictures to be found to enhance the lesson.

Pentecost

The day of Pentecost brings the Easter season to a climactic finale. It occurs fifty days after the resurrection. It is a time to remember God's gift of the Holy Spirit to the Church. It reminds us that Christ left us on this planet to carry out his will to tell the Good News to all the world.

IDEAS FOR CELEBRATING PENTECOST: Purchase red plastic Solo brand cups and use the tip of a hot glue gun to make a small hole in the center of the bottom. Secure the end of an eighteen-inch strip of ribbon inside the cup (tape it to a small piece of poster board) and then run the ribbon out the hole in the bottom of the cup. Tie the other end of the ribbon to the end of a stick or dowel. Cut strips of red, orange, and yellow crepe paper about 18 inches long. Then cut the strips in half lengthwise. Put a strip of double-faced tape (sticky on both sides) around the inside of the rim of the cup. Tape the strips of crepe paper, alternating colors, around the cup. The children may join in the morning's processional, twirling their "whishers." It makes for a joyous sight and a wonderful wind sound.

Ordinary Time

Next, the church enters a period of Ordinary Time. It begins the day after Pentecost and lasts until the Saturday before the first Sunday of Advent. (See chart of summary of the Church Year, Church Year Resource #3.)

It has been suggested that if one learns and participates in the movement and celebration of the Church Year, one has also "mastered" the order of worship.

> Advent and Lent—times of preparation, confession, and repentance.
>
> Christmas and Eastertide—times of proclamation and Good News.
>
> Epiphany, Pentecost, and Ordinary Time—times of commitment, dedication, and service.

The PREM (Presbyterian Reformed Educational Ministry) curriculum of the Presbyterian Church U.S.A. offers two sets of materials – *Bible Discovery* and *Celebrate* – which use the Church Year as framework for organizing its content.

Books:

A Rainbow of Seasons: A Leader's Resource for Living the Church Year by Sharon Lee. Minneapolis: Augsburg Publishing House, 1983.

Celebrating Holidays and Holy Days in Church and Family Settings by Judy Weaver. Nashville: Discipleship Resources, 1989.

Celebrating the Seasons with Children by Philip E. Johnson. New York: Pilgrim Press, 1984.

Celebrating Special Days in the Church School Year by Judy Gattis Smith. Colorado Springs: Meriwether Publishing Ltd., 1981.

Celebrating Through the Church Year by Betty McLaney. PREM Curriculum *Celebrate for Ages Birth to Two* (Parent Book), 1988.

Church Year Guide by Paul Bosch. Minneapolis: Augsburg Publishing House, 1987.

Family Worship Through the Year: Ideas for Every Season, Special Days and Holidays by Kristen Johnson Ingram. Valley Forge: Judson Press, 1984.

Follow the Year: A Family Celebration of Christian Holidays by Mala Powers. San Francisco: Harper and Row, 1985.

Handbook on the Christian Year by Hickman, Saliers, Stookey, and White. Nashville: Abingdon Press, 1986.

Remembering: God's People Celebrate Special Days and Times. JED Themepak.

Seasons to Remember: A Family Devotional and Activity Guide. Philadelphia: Fortress Press, 1982.

Seasons of God's Love—The Church Year by Jeanne Fogle. Philadelphia: Geneva Press, 1988.

Sprung Time: Seasons of the Christian Year by Robert G. Hamerton-Kelly. Nashville: The Upper Room, 1980.

Teaching with Music Through the Church Year by Judy Gattis Smith. Nashville: Abingdon Press, 1976.

The Year of the Lord by Theodore J. Kleinhans. St. Louis: Concordia Publishing House, 1967.

Through the Christian Year by Paul J. Philibert. Nashville: Abingdon Press, 1983.

To Celebrate: Reshaping Holidays and Rites of Passage. Ellenwood, Ga.: Alternatives, 1987.

Why Not Celebrate! by Sara Wenger Shenk. Intercourse, Pa.: Good Books, 1987.

Training Design:
"Learning and Celebrating Through the Year": Packet 2 Teacher/Leader Education Packets. Louisville: Presbyterian Church (U.S.A.)

Games:
"Christian Year Game" in *God's People Worship* (Course 4, Session 25:14) by Carolyn Brown. Youth Club Program, Inc. (Logos), Pittsburgh, 1989.

"Days and Seasons Game" in *Teaching and Celebrating Lent-Easter* by Pat and Don Griggs. Nashville: Abingdon.

"New Year Bingo" in *Celebrate Curriculum* Year 3 Elementary Teaching Kit for Grades 1–6. Louisville: Presbyterian Publishing House.

"In Quest of Church Seasons" by Anna Kay Baker. Jackson, Michigan: Fig Tree Enterprises, 3317 Carlton Blvd.

Adapt "Twister" by making an overlay of Church Year symbols.

A-V Resources:
Filmstrip: *The Church Year*. Celebrate Year 1. Elementary Teaching Kit for Grades 1–6. Louisville: Presbyterian Publishing House.

Filmstrip: *Living the Church Year* by John and Mary Harrell. Source: NTEP.

Videostrip: Christian Year. Cathedral Films.

Catalog :
EMI Quarterly from Educational Ministries, Inc., 2861–C Saturn St., Brea, CA 92621-6227.

Church Year Resource #1

CHURCH YEAR HOPSCOTCH

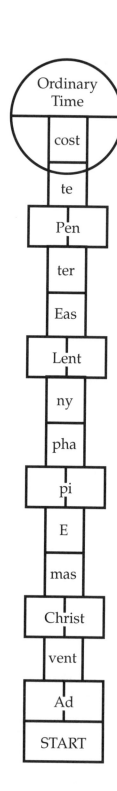

Ordinary Time

cost

te

Pen

ter

Eas

Lent

ny

pha

pi

E

mas

Christ

vent

Ad

START

INSTRUCTIONS:

1. Make a hopscotch game using chalk on concrete or masking tape on carpet or flooring.

2. Each player needs a small beanbag or a rock. These could be made or painted in the colors of the Church Year: purple, red, white, and green.

3. Go over the names of the seasons of the Church Year (Advent, Christmas, Epiphany, Lent, Easter, Pentecost, Ordinary Time). Pronounce each name with the accent on the syllable in the double squares. Discuss briefly what each season represents.

4. To play the game, players (one at a time) take their rock (or beanbag) and stand on Start. They throw the rock, trying to get it to land on one of the squares of the game. If they miss, they must wait for another turn. If they get it on a square, they then hop to that square. Hop on one foot for one square and two feet for the double squares. The group should chant the names of the seasons as the players hop toward Ordinary Time.

5. If the players lose their balance, it means returning to wait for another turn. If not, they must stand on one foot in the square containing the rock. If the rock can successfully be retrieved, the players may continue throwing and hopping to Ordinary Time and then back to Start.